# A Farewell Waltz

# A Farewell Waltz

Two Women and Their Arduous Exodus
from Nazi Germany

## Nicholas H Sommers

# Introduction

On a brisk March day in 1937 two women walked a bit fear-fully toward the Gestapo headquarters in Baden-Baden. Clouds had gathered over this world-famous spa town and a great deal had changed. Wealthy Jewish Americans had cut short their vacations when confronted with ominous threats and signs indicating they were no longer wanted. It was not only the foreigners, but also a minority of Germans who were now strangers in their own land.

The younger woman was 31, the older woman was 57. They were mother and daughter on the threshold of leaving Germany. Earlier that morning they had been at the Revenue Office and then at the police station. They had received their good conduct certificate which was a necessary requirement for leaving Germany and a necessary requirement for a visa to the United States. The U.S. Immigration Act of 1917 had an LPC clause (likely to become a public charge) and demanded a police affidavit attesting to the good character of the immigrant. The U.S. Undersecretary of State Phillips in August of 1933 had advised that "the consul is only concerned with determining in a helpful and considerate manner whether the applicant for the visa have met the requirements of the law."

1

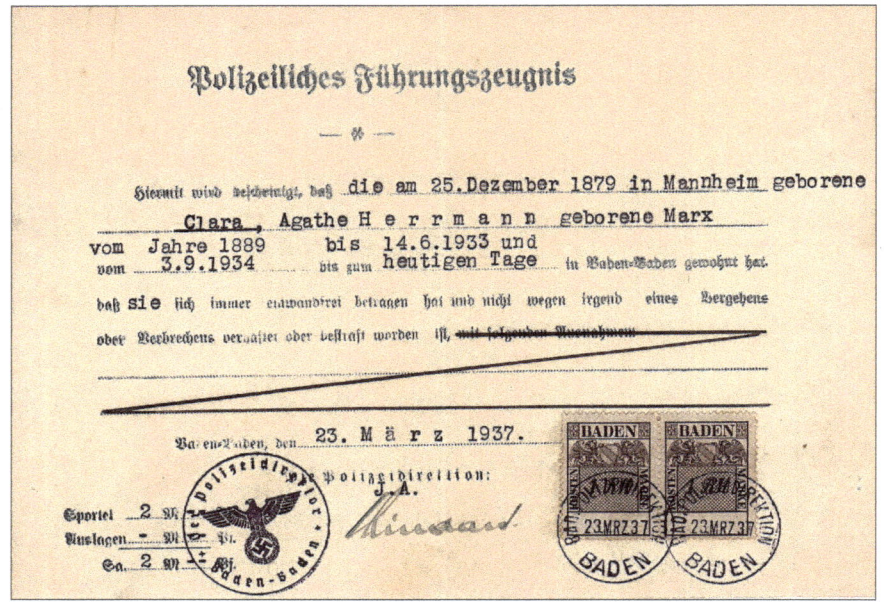

The older woman's certificate states that *Clara Agathe Herrmann has lived in Baden-Baden from 1889 till June 14, 1933, and from September 3, 1934, until the present day. She has always acted correctly and never been convicted of any crime.* Two stamps affixed to the document indicate that two Marks have been paid and there is a stamp with the swastika logo along with a signature of the police director.

At the police station they are told that before they can pick up their passports, they are to report to the Gestapo at 4:00 p.m. This is the story of the events leading up to that fateful day and the tragedy that enveloped my family in the Third Reich....

As a small boy I had often wondered why my family hadn't left Germany earlier. What had made them so reviled? Why did it take them so long to get out? How could a nation of Bach, Beethoven and Brahms have produced a nation of Hitler, Himmler and Hoess?

My grandmother never spoke of her experiences and my mother only briefly mentioned her own. This story would never have come to pass if I hadn't found an old file folder in a forgotten desk drawer which contained letters written from jail by my mother and grandmother--a series of letters covering the period of 1933 till the summer of 1942. These letters served as a catalyst. They helped me uncover my own distant ancestors using all the available aids of today including the internet, a DNA genome project, uncovering archives in Munich and revisiting sites in Germany and The Czech Republic.

All the main actors in this drama are now dead. My grandmother used to say, "You can tell the truth about the dead." That gives me the courage to write their story. Someone once said that a story once told never dies. Perhaps that is too much to hope for. Let the reader be the judge.

# The First Reich

**M**y ancestors arrived in the Rhine River valley from Italy sometime between the 9th and 10th century which was roughly one thousand years before there was a state of Germany. This was shortly after Charlemagne (Karl der Grosse) had been crowned Roman Emperor in 800 A.D. Later it was to become The Holy Roman Empire, which was neither Holy nor Roman nor an Empire, but a loose confederation of principalities, dukedoms, and other assorted noble estates. They were primarily German-speaking states.

Charlemagne established several of the leitmotifs of this Rhineland culture, a culture of intolerance and xenophobia of swordsmanship and scholarship. It was Charlemagne who in 782 ordered 4500 Saxons beheaded at Verden when they refused to convert to Christianity. Shortly thereafter Pope Leo III crowned him Roman Emperor. While Charlemagne relied on the power of the sword, he also encouraged scholars at his court. He was reported to have been learning how to read on his deathbed and instilled a love of learning in his children and grandchildren. He had writing standardized by establishing the Carolingian miniscule, a standard way of writing small letters. The Holy Roman Empire he founded was the First Reich and lasted for about a thousand years until its dissolution in 1806.

Sometime in the tenth century, Otto I, later The Holy Roman Emperor, described as a prince of education and letters, invited a noted Jewish scholarly family to move to the Rhineland from Lucca which was a Tuscan city in north-central Italy. (The northern part of what we call Italy was at that time called Lombardy and a part of the Holy Roman Empire.) The Kalonymus family and their entourage settled in the area of Worms and Speyer on the west bank of the Rhine in an area that is today known as the Rhineland-Palatinate. Then as now it was an important wine-growing region. The Jews in the area were not only teachers and scholars but also vintners and traders. Through their correspondence and trading they had contacts throughout Europe and the Near East. They were heavily taxed for the privilege of living there. It was a form of early protection money. In exchange for their taxes, they were protected (most of the time) by the Emperor, King or Elector and Archbishop. Through their contacts and economic activities, they were seen by the nobles as important contributors to the local economy.

For hundreds of years relationships between Jews and their Christian and pagan neighbors was fairly harmonious. During that time there were a number of royal decrees granting Jews trading privileges and royal protection. The Synod of Mainz at the beginning of the tenth century declared that anyone who slays a Jew is to be treated as a murderer. While their livelihood was protected their lives were still precarious. Much of their activity was proscribed. After a certain hour they had to return to their ghetto, a walled in part of the town. They could not own a sword or carry any kind of arms. Permission of the local lord was required for them to settle in a community. When Bishop Rudiger Huzmann wanted to build a large cathedral in Speyer in the beginning of the 10th century, he

discovered that masons from Italy were expensive, and his own funds were limited. His solution was to invite Jews to come to Speyer so that their tax revenues could be used to finance the cathedral. The bishop extends them protection and privileges that some viewed as better than those afforded Christians. By this time the area of Speyer, Worms and Mainz had become a religious as well as intellectual center of Jewish learning. Most of the larger cities have Jewish streets close to the cathedral. In 1074 Jews and other citizens of Worms are given custom privileges by Emperor Henry IV. In 1090 these privileges are extended to the Jews of Speyer.

The golden age of Rhineland Jewry was quickly coming to an end. In 1095 the byzantine emperor Alexios I. Komnenos requests military help from Pope Urban II. The Turks and Arabs were on the move in the Middle East and killing Christians in the Holy Land. On November 27, 1095, in Clermont the pope preaches a crusade against the infidels unintentionally perhaps, creating an unbridgeable rift between Christians and Jews.

As the crusaders headed off to the Holy Land in 1096 there were some who decided it was easy to kill the infidels in their midst. Thus, a ragtag army of peasant crusaders led by Emicho of Leiningen, and another army led by Peter the Hermit go up and down the Rhine valley killing 800 Jews in Worms, another 1000 or so in Mainz, and an untold number in other communities from Xanten to Cologne and Trier. They burn synagogues and books and plunder the homes of the Jews. In Speyer the Jews are protected by the bishop who harbors them in his palace. The majority of Jews, when told to convert or die, in an echo of Charlemagne, chose death using the only weapon they have which are the ritual slaughter knives they use on animals. Husbands first slit their wives' throats and then their children's before committing suicide. Some Jews escaped and a few converted under duress.

The next year, in 1097, Henry IV asks the Jews who escaped, including those who had been forcibly baptized, to come back and resettle the Rhineland. Although they make up less than one per cent of the population, they are important traders and craftsmen. They are also the principal money lenders since the Catholic Church has given them the monopoly by forbidding money lending with interest. From now on, throughout the Middle Ages, there will be periods of expulsion and return.

Hatred of Jews was now official dogma. Anti-Judaism becomes part of the infrastructure of Christianity. In an essentially illiterate society this dogma was cast in stone in cathedral carvings. As people entered their cathedrals, they could see devilish gargoyles wearing pointed Jewish hats. In Strassburg one of the cathedral capitals has a Judensau, a popular medieval representation showing Jews as suckling a pig or eating its excrement. This hatred becomes part of the Catholic Church. In 1179 and again in 1215 the church's Lateran

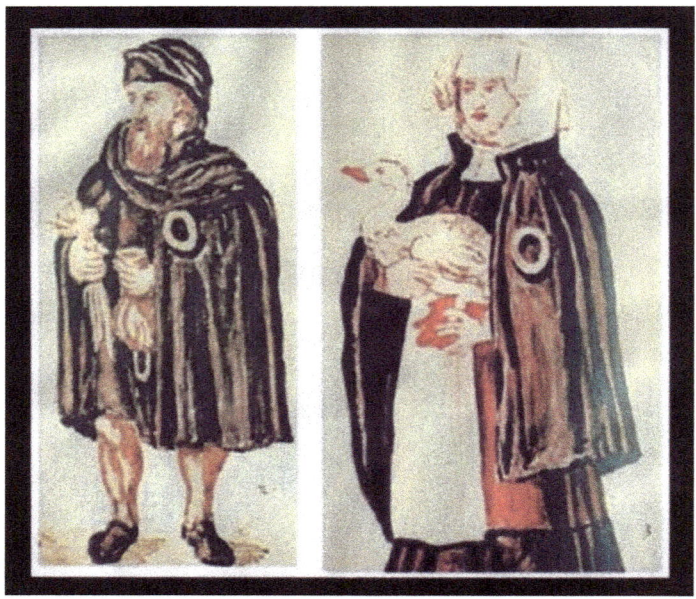

Council declared that Jews may not employ Christian servants and their clothing should carry identifying badges. In Germany this became a large yellow ring the size of a plate. They also had to wear a pointed hat. In 1240 during the reign of Pope Gregory IX, the Church officially decreed the Talmud heretical, blasphemous and a threat to Christian faith. In 1242 cartloads of volumes are publicly burned. In 1306 the Jews are expelled from France.

In the 14th century Jews were accused of being responsible for the Black Death. While there may have been fewer deaths in the Jewish population due to better hygiene, time has proven these scurrilous accusations false as the plague was carried by fleas. In many communities Jews are burned in their homes. On February 14, 1394, thousands of Jews are driven out of Strassburg and murdered. It is important to note that in all records from the time, there isn't a single record of a Jew raising arms against a Christian.

Time and again my ancestors were driven away from the Rhine valley that had been their home for centuries. The expulsions erased any debts that Christians owed to Jews. This "positive" effect was not enough to overcome the negative effect the expulsions had on the local economy. While the peasantry might have been pleased, the local lords couldn't be as their tax coffers were diminished.

As the Middle Ages waned, German guilds grew in importance. The guilds were cartel organizations which kept tight control of prices and even established the German purity of products. One such guild, the beer brewers of Bavaria established a Reinheitsgebot or purity law which regulated the quality of beer brewed in Germany. It could only contain water, barley, and hops. This law which was not repealed until 1993 kept non-German beers from being sold in German speaking lands. It goes without saying that Jews were also prohibited from joining any guilds.

In 1543 Martin Luther, the arch enemy of Catholicism, echoes Charlemagne's intolerance when he writes in his pamphlet "On Jews and Their Lies" that the synagogues and schools be set on fire, prayer books destroyed, rabbis forbidden to preach, homes razed, and property and money confiscated. If this sounds

like a recipe for Hitler to follow, it was. Hitler read this publication of Luther's while in prison in 1928 writing "Mein Kampf". In another publication, "Vom Schemhamphoras und vom Geschlecht Christi", Luther writes of his remembrance of the images in his parish church: "Here in Wittemberg, in our parish church, there is a sow carved in stone under which lie young pigs and Jews who are suckling: behind the sow stands a rabbi who is lifting the leg of the sow [who] bows down and looks with great effort into the Talmud under the sow.." While Luther may be seen as the anti-Catholic cleric he none-the-less carries with him the Catholic anti-Jewish images of his youth, a culture by now deeply ingrained in the fabric of the German speaking lands.

During this time my ancestors moved from the Rhineland eastwards into Poland and Silesia. For a brief period of time in the early 17th century they settled in Nikolsburg, now known as Mikulov, on the Austrian border with Moravia. The Counts of Liechtenstein and later the Dietrichsteins welcomed the influx of Jewish traders and merchants. Franz Cardinal von Dietrichstein was a true Renaissance prince who granted them greater liberties by removing them from the jurisdiction of the municipal courts to the feudal court and by allowing them to trade in wine. His successor, Maximilian of Dietrichstein allowed the Jews to receive shelter inside the town walls during war for a fee. Nikolsburg at this time has also become one of the most important centers of Jewish learning with more than 300 students in its yeshivas or schools. Gershon Aschkenazi (literally Gershon the German), one of my ancestors becomes Chief Rabbi of Moravia.

By the mid-17th century, with the decimation caused by the thirty years war, the German nobles who only recently had expelled the Jews, begged them to return. At this time my ancestors moved from Nikolsburg to Mussbach back to the Rhineland-Palatinate.

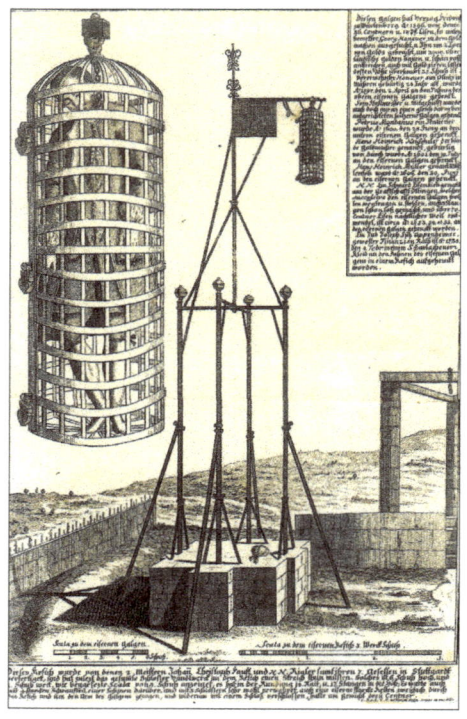

They were needed both to repopulate the devastated areas as well as to provide a greater tax base. At that time the nobles also encouraged and created a new class of "court Jews" who became essential financiers and expanded royal coffers. Notable among these are Samson Wertheimer who was court banker to three Holy Roman Emperors and Joseph Suess Oppenheimer who becomes financier to the Duke of Wuerttemberg. The duke was extremely grateful for the help Oppenheimer provided and much to the chagrin of the duke's many enemies and the general populace he heaped rewards and praise on his court Jew.

In 1737 the Duke of Wuerttemberg suddenly dies. Immediately after his death Oppenheimer is arrested (as are all the Jews of Stuttgart) and charged with fraud, embezzlement, bribery, and lecherous conduct with court ladies. He is tried and convicted. Offered the opportunity to convert to Christianity he refuses and is hung in a gibbet, a bird cage structure, and his body hangs there above the town square left to rot for six years, a constant reminder to the populace of his alleged crimes. Today historians agree that it was judicial murder. In 1940 the Nazis produced an infamous propaganda film entitled Jud Suess which celebrated the 18th century trial.

By 1750 my ancestors had moved to another small rural community near Mussbach called Venningen which is situated along the southern wine road of the Pfalz. There they were merchants, vintners, butchers, and rabbis. For them there was safety in a rural area. Although there were still many proscriptions on what they could and could not do, they lived in harmony with their neighbors.

The seventeenth and eighteenth century were periods of enlightenment and the Jewish communities along the Rhine prospered. As a result of the French Revolution, liberty, equality, and fraternity reached the shores of the Rhine when Napoleon added the Departement du Mont-Tonnere to the French Republic. The whole of the Palatinate was under French rule from 1797 to 1814 and with it came the emancipation of the Jews. They could now be full-fledged citizens. Patronymic names were no longer allowed, and everyone had to be listed in the census with a surname. Thus, Gershon son of Jacob chose the name of Jakob Teutsch I on March 11, 1808. Another brother, who also lived in Venningen, took the name of Joseph Teutsch. By this time the first Reich had come to an end.

# The Inter Regnum
# and the Second Reich

The emancipation in the area did not survive the Congress of Vienna in 1815. After Napoleon's defeat the Southern Rhineland was given to conservative Bavaria as the Pfalz. While liberalism had taken hold in the area, the status of Jews was reversed. German romanticism and nationalism were on the rise. German writers, scientists and musicians began to extol the virtues of the German people. Religious persecution was replaced by racial persecution. Writers, philosophers, scientists and musicians rail against Jewish influence in society. In 1850 Richard Wagner writes a polemic about Judaism in Music.

In 1871, after the Franco-Prussian War, the 300 separate states, principalities and free cities are united into modern Germany by Bismarck. The time of the Kaiser, 1871 to 1917, is known as the Second Reich. Jews are now emancipated and made equal citizens. The attacks however do not stop. In 1873 Wilhelm Marr, a journalist, coins the term Anti-Semitism and founds the league for Anti-Semitism in 1879. Numerous publications appear extolling the Aryan race with particular emphasis on the Germanic race and its purity. In 1892 the Jewish cemetery in Wachenheim, where ancestors of mine from the 17<sup>th</sup> and 18<sup>th</sup> century are buried, is vandalized. In 1897 the Jewish cemetery in Kuppenheim near Baden-Baden is repeatedly vandalized. Huston Chamberlin, the son-in-law of Richard Wagner, writes a book, The basis of the 19<sup>th</sup> century (Die Grundlagen des 19. Jahrhunderts) which espouses Arianism and hatred of Jews. In 1900, Kaiser Wilhelm recommends the book be made part of the gymnasium curriculum.

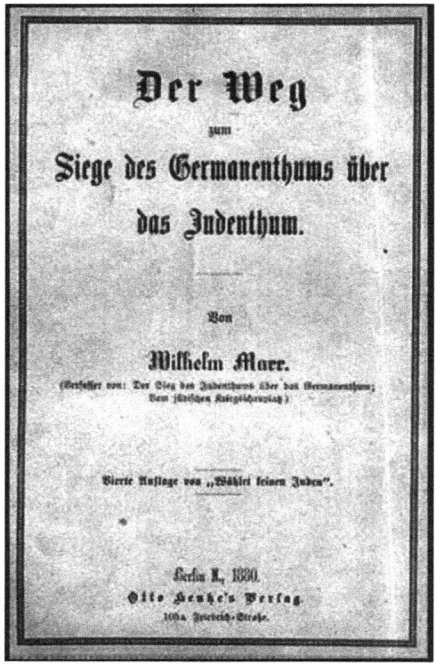

For a brief period, the Jews of Germany are allowed to attend universities. They quickly rise to prominence as doctors, lawyers, scientists, academics, and preeminent merchants. After World War I Germany is given its first democracy during the Weimar Republic. The majority of the government bureaucrats remain staunchly conservative yearning for the autocratic rulers of the past. The judiciary remains perhaps the most conservative of all. Many are upset by the rising prominence of Jewish professionals in law, medicine, and science. Periodically there are outbursts of anti-Semitism. Both in 1921 and 1923 Adolph Hitler was already in the news: first for disrupting a meeting of the Bayernbund and later in the famous Beer Hall Putsch where he railed against the "Jew Berlin" government. In 1928, forty-two gravestones in the Jewish cemetery in Essingen are destroyed, including that of Jakob Teutsch I, a monument that is immediately rebuilt.

In eleven hundred years the Rhineland develops a culture of intolerance towards outsiders. The echoes of Charlemagne's laws Capitulatio de Partibus Saxonae which proscribed brutal and violent repression of non-believers and specified death, high fines or slavery for infringements of the law found reprises again and again in German speaking lands. The idea of purity was expanded from products to people. While geopolitical causes for the rise of the National Socialists are well known less has been written about the Rhineland culture which nourished its ideology and provided the fertile ground for Nazi excesses.

The day after Hitler was appointed chancellor by President Hindenburg, Hitler was given the authority to dissolve the Reichstag (the German Parliament) which then paved the way for a number of decrees. The Decree for the Protection of the German People was followed on February 28, 1933, with the Reichstag Fire Decree, "Decree for the Protection of the People and the State". In this decree, as Ian Kershaw has written, Hitler is given "the right to commit murder without a trial [thereby] substituting murder for rule of law." While these decrees were aimed to nullify any opposition, at the same time, as Ingo Mueller has written, they "annulled almost all the basic rights guaranteed by the constitution" and paved the way for the wave of anti-Semitic laws which were to follow. The Germans had become legal atheists. They used the law but didn't believe in it. This was in evidence in their People's Courts (Volksgericht) and in their Special Courts (Sondergericht).

This was the milieu in which my grandfather and grandmother grew up and which influenced and inalterably changed the life of my grandmother, mother and uncle.

# The Emancipation

My grandfather, Carl Theodore Herrmann, was born in the small rural village of Venningen in the Bavarian Pfalz (Palatinate) in 1863. His mother was Agathe Teutsch. (Both of my grandmother's grandmothers were Teutsch sisters, Frederike and Agathe Teutsch.) The family had lived in that area for centuries with of course periodic expulsions. They were livestock dealers, farmers, traders, butchers, and vintners for generations. Many ancestors were rabbis. With the emancipation of 1871, a larger world opened. My grandfather's brother Ernst became the first in his family to attend university, obtain a JD degree and became an attorney in Baden-Baden. Carl headed for Baden-Baden in about 1885 to join his brother and sister.

People were drawn to Baden-Baden not only by its famous mineral springs and baths which were founded by the Romans more than two thousand years ago, but also by its casino. Although there had been gambling in the city for many years, the big growth spurt came when The French Government, under Louis Phillipe, the Citizen King, banned gambling in 1837. Jacques Benezet who had held the concession for gambling in The Palais Royal quarter had to find a new venue and found it across the Rhine in Baden. Special trains came directly from Paris. Now well to do socialites and aristocrats

flocked across the Rhine to the city. Benezet also built the grand horse racing course at Iffizheim near Baden, a track which was run by The Jockey Club of Paris. His son Eduard Benezet built the present- day casino in1855 and had Franz Liszt and other prominent composers perform as a way of increasing the cultural renown of the city. The town had become a magnet for the well to do and functioned as their summer capital. The nearby international horse races at Iffizheim, the manicured parkways and promenades along the tiny stream Oos along with attractive villas and hiking paths through the Black Forest to romantic vistas and castle ruins made the town an idyllic destination.

The residents of Baden hesitated to admit Jews as full-time residents. In 1862 even Baron Rothschild was denied residency in Baden-Baden by the town's inhabitants. Shortly thereafter the Duchy of Baden emancipates its Jews. By 1865 18 Jews are listed as inhabitants equaling 0.2% of the population.

Royalty often resided in Baden-Baden. Kaiser Wilhelm I came every summer for forty years. The Prince of Wales, Queen Victoria, Russian counts and princes, the King of Wuerttemberg, Napoleon

III, and other reigning monarchs met there. Artists, authors, and musicians also came. Dostoyevski, Turgenev, Berlioz, and Brahms, were all resident at one time. In 1863 Dostoyevski, a notorious gambler himself, writes a novella *The Gambler* based on his experiences at the roulette table in the Baden-Baden casino. During the Franco-Prussian war of 1870 and following the establishment of the German Empire in 1871 gambling came to an end. The French no longer came, and Baden relied on its thermal baths, pure air and proximity to the Black Forest to continue to draw visitors. In 1883 the Prince of Wales came for the 25th anniversary of the International Races at Iffizheim and his presence gave a new impetus to the elite to return to Baden.

With the complete emancipation of Jews which was ensured in article 3 of the German Constitution in 1871, they were finally free to move about. While still in high school my grandfather, Carl Theodore Herrmann, started to collect postage stamps a new hobby since postage stamps were first introduced in the German area in 1850. He turned his hobby into a business and began to sell and trade stamps. Venningen with a population of about 900 was not a good location but the lure of Baden with its international clientele seemed ideal. With a population of about 12000 the town must have seemed like a big city to the country boy from Venningen. It was a good choice and Carl's business prospered. He started out by selling stamps but also began to represent The New York Life Insurance Company selling insurance policies to the wealthy visitors. He had amassed a small amount of capital by 1891 and together with a partner opened a private bank doing business as Carl T. Herrmann & Co. By this time two sisters and a brother were also established in Baden-Baden. His brother Ernst was an attorney. One sister owned a shoe store while the other was married to a hotelier.

Freed from the constraints of rural Venningen, Carl assimilated into the life and culture of Baden. He was very much a secular Jew and supported the Reform movement in Judaism. Together with his brother he helped raise funds for a Synagogue in Baden. They commissioned the architect Professor Ludwig Levy in nearby Karlsruhe. The synagogue was to have none of the middle eastern character of older synagogues but rather mimicked the neo-Romanesque Christian churches in places like Speyer, Worms and Mainz. Architecturally the synagogue reflected the degree of assimilation of the Baden-Baden Jews.

It was a sunny day in August 1899 when the synagogue was officially opened and dedicated. Representatives of the Grand Duke of Baden, the mayor and town councilors, Christian church dignitaries, rabbis and important city fathers were present. Rabbi Julius Mayer spoke about the love that the Jewish inhabitants of Baden had for The Fatherland, Kaiser and the Empire (Reich). The Grand duke's representative said that the synagogue would become an important addition to the city and hoped that peace and blessings would flow from it. Thereafter the Tora was brought into the synagogue. Afterwards at the evening festivities attorney Dr. Ernst Herrmann opened the evening with words of welcome and thanks to all who had come. His words were echoed by Banker Herrmann. The evening closed when Dr. Herrmann raised his glass to Rabbi Julius Mayer and thanked him and his predecessor Moritz Rothschild.

This is the same year that Houston Stewart Chamberlain, the British born German philosopher publishes his *Die Grundlagen des neunzehnten Jahrhunderts*, The Foundations of the Nineteenth Century. In it he espoused German/Aryan racial superiority and the kind of antisemitism that led to Nazi racial ideas. Kaiser Wilhelm II recommended that the book be part of German gymnasiums. Hitler was greatly influenced by this publication and the fact that Houston was married to Wagner's daughter.

By 1898 my grandfather was engaged to my grandmother, and they were married in 1899. It was probably an arranged marriage as they were related via the Teutsch clan. The importance of my grandfather can be seen in an etching made at this time by a prominent artist named Ismael Gentz which he dedicated to Bankier Carl T. Herrmann. It shows my grandmother and grandfather promenading near the casino in Baden-Baden. Gentz specialized in paintings of professionals and industrialists. One of his best- known sketches may be that of Edgar Allan Poe which adorns the first page of many of Poe's books.

# Life in Baden-Baden

At the beginning of the twentieth century, within the space of a few months between November 1900 and February 1901, two boys were born in Baden-Baden, the one to a devout Catholic family, the other to a secular Jewish family. Their lives will mirror the fate of their country though they probably never met in Baden-Baden. Rudolph Franz Ferdinand Hoess was born on the outskirts of town at the end of November 1900. His father was a shopkeeper selling tea and coffee. He ruled the family with strict discipline and hoped that his son would become a priest. When Rudolph is six the family moves away from Baden-Baden. His father dies when Rudolph is 14.

Bruno Willy Herrmann, born in February 1901, was the first child of Carl Theodore and Klara Herrmann. Overjoyed at their new son they decide to purchase a house with a large garden. The house they purchase, Schillerstrasse 19, is strategically situated across from the Brenner Park Hotel and contains a large garden extending to the corner. To help with the household they hire a faithful factotum, Marie who is a bit older than Klara. Now that Jews could go to university, they hoped that their son would enter one of the professions like law, medicine, or teaching. The century had opened with great optimism.

In 1904 Carl T. Herrmann is a guest of The New York Life Insurance Company as he was a member of what was then called the $200,000 club. ($200,000 in 1904 would have an equivalent value of over $5,000,000 today) He traveled to New York and then proceeded to West Baden Springs in Indiana, to the St. Louis World's Fair, to Chicago and back to New York.

In March1905 Carl and Klara are overjoyed at the birth of their second child, Edith. Carl is so proud that he names the house on Schillerstrasse 19, Villa Edith. A large brass plaque is affixed to the house joining a custom of other villas in the area. A large veranda with stone balusters extends outside the master bedroom on the second floor. It is filled with planters of red geraniums. Above it, extending from the third- floor window, there is a smaller wooden balcony. The multi-gabled roof is adorned with intricate wooden carvings. A large foyer welcomes visitors. A few steps up and to the right there is a music room with a grand piano and large windows overlooking the Lichtenthaler Alle, the beautifully landscaped promenade along

Baden-Baden, Villa Edith.

the little stream the Oss. A dining room and kitchen complete the first floor. On the second floor, above the music room, there is the conservatory where palms and other exotic plants are cultivated. A stone veranda outside the conservatory is used for breakfasts in the warmer months. There are a number of bedrooms for the family and guests. The third floor has a sewing room, a small apartment for the household help and storage space. Behind the house there is a garage with sleeping quarters above for the chauffeur and a dovecote. The property has a large garden extending to the corner.

The house is ideal for entertaining. A steady stream of visitors and clients enjoy the hospitality of Villa Edith. Prominent authors Arthur Schnitzler and Stefan Zweig, composers and musicians Leo Blech and the Friedberg, Flesch, Becker trio, White Russian aristocrat Count Alexander Shuvalov and Baron Le Jeune, politicians and ambassadors including Hans Morgenthau visit Villa Edith. There are wealthy Americans. It was the gilded age. One woman in particular fascinated little Edith. The woman wore a blue and white brocade dress whose buttons were a row of diamond and sapphire broaches. When Edith admired the dress, the woman gave her one of the buttons. Little Edith has an autograph book and asks visitors for their autographs.

In 1913 Carl purchases an Oldsmobile convertible touring car. It is the same year that he is a VIP guest on the maiden voyage of the Zeppelin Sachsen. In the picture he can be seen in the third

window from the left with the light-colored hat. Shortly thereafter World War I breaks out. The family is patriotic and loyal to the monarchy partly in an urge to assimilate as quickly as possible, partly because of the historic symbiotic relationship between the Jews and the royal courts. During the war the Carl T. Herrmann bank donates an ambulance to the Red Cross.

Meanwhile, Rudolph Franz Ferdinand Hoess whose father has died runs away from home. At the age of 14 he first works in an army hospital and then joins the German Army in his father's old regiment. He fights in Turkey and by the end of the war has risen to the rank of sergeant at the age of 17, the youngest non-commissioned officer in the army.

All three male nephews of Carl who are old enough to fight die during the war. One falls near Reims in 1914, one falls in Priesterwald in 1915 and one dies from the great influenza epidemic in LaRoche in the closing days of the war in 1918. In 1919 Carl T. Herrmann is elected (Stadtrat) alderman of Baden-Baden running as a candidate of the Social Democratic Party.

# The Weimar Republic

During this time period of growing inflation, the majority of the garden property is sold, and a small hotel/pension is built on the land. The hotel is known as Haus National and is run by the former chef of the King of Wuerttemberg. Edith is apprenticed to the chef so that she may learn how to cook and supervise household staff since her father decided these were important future skills.

As the constitutional convention in Weimar begins, the terrific debt burden of the war has already created a quickening pace of inflation. The war was never financed through taxes but by printing money. By the time the First World War ended the average German's savings were worth 50% of what they were at the beginning of the war. Only those who owned foreign shares or had money in foreign banks (which was technically illegal) were able to survive the inflationary period. The worst time was 1922/1923. People were paid every day in the morning and quickly ran out to buy items before the prices rose again. By 1922 a loaf of bread cost 163 marks and during the height of hyperinflation it cost as much as 200,000,000,000 marks.

By this time Willy has entered university and begun his medical studies. He graduates from the University of Frankfurt in 1924 writing his doctoral dissertation on cancerous polyps of the colon.

Before settling down in Baden-Baden as a pediatrician, he works as a ship surgeon on a voyage around Africa to Japan and back.

Meanwhile Rudolph Hoess has renounced his membership in the Catholic Church and joined the Freikorps Rossbach in the Baltic area. The Freikorps was a paramilitary group

Dissertation der Medizinischen Fakultät zu Frankfurt a. M.
Juli 1924.

Nr. 804

Aus dem Senckenbergischen Pathologischen Institut
der Universität zu Frankfurt a. M.
(Direktor: Prof. B. Fischer)

**Ueber Krebsbildung auf Darmpolypen**

von

**Willy Herrmann**

Medizinalpraktikant aus Baden-Baden.

Zusammenfassung.

1. Polyposis intestinalis ist eine praecanceröse Erkrankung.
2. Die Tatsache des häufigen erblichen und familiären Auftretens der Polyposis beweist, daß der Determinationsfaktor der Geschwulstbildung in einer primären Gewebsmißbildung liegt.
3. Es wird ein Fall von ausgedehnter Polyposis des Rectums bei einem 35 jährigen Manne mitgeteilt, bei dem die Umwandlung zahlreicher Polypen in Carcinom nachzuweisen war.

Referent: Prof. Dr. Fischer.

made up of former soldiers. They fought primarily against communists but also against the French occupiers of the Ruhr. In 1923 Hoess joins the Nazi Party after hearing Hitler speak. This is the same year that Hoess is arrested as being the ringleader of a group which at the instigation of Martin Borman kills a local schoolteacher, Walter Kadow. Kadow was suspected of having informed on a Freikorps member who was planning to sabotage French supply lines. Hoess is sentenced to 10 years in Brandenburg prison.

In 1925 at the age of 62, Carl T. Herrmann dies. He leaves his family in good financial shape. There are no mortgages on either Villa Edith (Schillerstrasse 19) or the villa he had given his daughter which is located up the hill on Fremersbergstrasse 10. He names his son Willy as executor of his will.

Germany is technically democratic now however its institutions, chiefly among them its judiciary and military, are still archly conservative. The judiciary still longs for the order that prevailed under the Kaiser while the military has not accepted the defeat of World War 1. The paramilitary Freikorps which has its roots under Frederick II of Prussia sees the communists and socialists as responsible for its defeat. They fight against the Bavarian Soviet Republic in 1919 and count among their members future prominent Nazi party men such as Borman, Himmler, and Hoess.

# Third Reich

…**I**t was another formality in the process of leaving Germany. They had their good conduct certificates and only needed their external passports which were all that was required by the U.S. consulate in Stuttgart. Klara (she wrote her name with a K) prized punctuality and order, two ingrained German qualities which explains why she told her daughter, Edith, that they mustn't be late for their appointment as they left their villa, Schillerstrasse 19, late on that fateful afternoon. Edith glanced at the brass plate next to the front door which identified the house as Villa Edith. Since her brother was in America, she and her mother were to sell the villas as soon as possible and join him. They had tried to leave 2 years ago but Edith had already been imprisoned in Gotteszell for seven months a year earlier due to false charges of currency manipulation. These charges had been the result of a denunciation by a tenant in her Fremersbergstrasse villa. She had given Fritz Koch a power of attorney to take care of her house while she was away since she and her mother were anticipating moving to America and had already stored furniture away and moved to the attic of her mother's house on Schillerstrasse. As a result of her incarceration her passport had already once been taken away. But all that was behind them, and they could look forward to a new beginning.

35

The two women walked to their appointment saying little, each engrossed in their own thoughts. Recently they had obtained permission from the police to buy shoes and clothing for their trip to America. Everything was in order. Klara was secretly suspicious. Karlsruhe was where the customs offices were located. The year before, while Edith was imprisoned, a man from the customs service had visited Villa Edith to have a look around. By now the Third Reich had become a system where personal allegiances to the Fuehrer were rewarded and ordinary citizens denounced neighbors to The Gestapo. The customs service and the Gestapo had been alerted by an informant, a man named Fritz Koch who was a tenant in Fremersberg 10, that a moving van had been seen in front of Edith's Fremersbergstrasse villa, in front of Villa Edith and in front of a warehouse. After having a look, the customs service inspector assured Klara that there was nothing to worry about. In the last year nothing further was heard.

When they entered the Gestapo offices, the officer in charge again told them that there was no political reason for them not to receive their passports, however the gentlemen standing nearby had a few questions. Klara looked at the grey suited figure and recognized him as the same person who had inspected her house the year before. He asked them to come with him to the Internal Revenue Offices (Finanzamt) and politely held the door open for the two women. The Internal Revenue offices were not far away and as they arrived another three men were waiting for them. They were all from the customs service in Karlsruhe. According to Edith, "after they took down all the personal information about us, they asked me to wait in a room downstairs while mother was to be questioned. It was 4:30 pm." Time passed. The only picture on the walls was a portrait of Hitler. With each hour Edith became more agitated. What was happening to her mother? At 8:30pm she asked to see her. "I felt so bad, they let me into the interrogation room, but since I was so close to fainting, they let me go home."

That night and the next day there was still no sign of Klara. Edith contacted everyone she thought might have some authority. The chief of the district court told her that her mother "has been placed in police detention, protective custody (Shutzhaft) for 2 times 24 hours which has now been extended to 3 times 24 hours." The judge and her attorney Mr. Roth tried to no avail to obtain release of her mother. Edith realizes "one is powerless against police detention." She had no idea why her mother was still being detained.

So much had changed since her father died. Edith remembered how her mother and brother had encouraged her to study voice after two disastrous arranged and annulled marriages. She studied voice in Milan with Maestro Piccoli and had even sung with Tito Schipa, finally making her debut as Margarete in Gounod's Faust. Her bohemian life was filled with weekend picnics along Lago Maggiore with all sorts of admirers. She lived down the block from Santa Maria delle Grazie where Leonardo painted The Last Supper. Since she already spoke French fluently it was easy to learn Italian and she loved the musical language. However, while her mother and brother had encouraged her musical studies, her mother did not think a career in the demi monde of the theater was proper for a banker's daughter. She had returned to Baden-Baden in late 1932. In January 1933 she went to Berlin to study singing Lieder with Konrad von Zawilowski a retired opera singer who had become a well- known voice teacher. These lessons were cut short by the advent of a new regime. In 1933 Adolph Hitler had come to power. Her brother left quickly for two reasons: first because he was a doctor and could no longer practice his profession and for a second darker reason unknown to his family.

At her mother's urging, Edith undertook a potentially hazardous trip from Baden-Baden to Strasbourg to bring her brother some Swiss francs and selected jewelry to take to the new world. It wasn't the first time she had been a "smuggler". She remembered one trip from Italy when she hid a turtle under her beret as a gift for Willy. The turtle behaved as they were inspected in their train compartment by the German customs officers. Thankfully her hat did not move. Her trip to and from Strasbourg was not without fear. She said goodbye to her brother who left for his first port of call, Santo Domingo. Passport control was uneventful, and the customs officers simply asked if she had anything to declare. Her handbag was a bit lighter now, nothing the customs officer could see.

In the months since her brother left, the new government had suspended constitutional protections and established the first concentration camp for political prisoners at Dachau. In April more laws were enacted to limit Jews from participating in public life. Klara and Edith were frightened when on April 1st a boycott was organized against Jewish owned stores. The book burning of May 1st while not the first in German speaking lands, was the first in recent memory. Like so many, they hoped these were only temporary measures and that the government would not last. With that in mind Klara planned a trip to Paris. Paris was a diversion. They had many friends there. It was cheap which was the reason so many expats, artists and writers called Paris home. Her mother's Good Conduct certificate noted the absence from June 14, 1933, till September 3, 1934. That was the time they left for Paris. Originally planned as a short visit, an unexpected problem occurred.

In Paris after a few weeks Klara started to cough up bits of blood and complained of chest pain. She spent a great deal of time resting. They ultimately visited Dr. Vulliet, at Avenue 6 General-Detrie. He diagnosed pneumococcal pneumonia and in the days before antibiotics, suggested that she leave for the south and warmer climates. They decided to go to Palma Mallorca so that her mother could rest and recuperate. Edith went to the bank and exchanged money for Spanish pesetas. Unknown to Edith, a German bank employee observed the exchange. It was the son-in-law of the tenant in her Fremersbergstrasse villa.

When they arrived in Palma, Edith placed an ad in the local paper for Spanish lessons. She was delighted to receive a host of offers including several marriage proposals. While she would have liked to have met some of them, her mother did not approve. None-the-less she learned Spanish from a charming instructor. They made many expat friends including May Butler-Ansay, an English woman with whom they corresponded for many years thereafter. As her mother's health improved the situation in Germany grew darker. The newspapers reported layers of laws which restricted the ability of Jews to earn a living. One law against habitual criminals allowed courts to order indefinite imprisonment. After President Hindenburg's death, Adolph Hitler had abolished the office of president and had named himself the Fuehrer, a dictatorial leader. As soon as Klara felt better, they decided to return to Baden-Baden and sell their villas. They wanted to join Willy as soon as possible but the barriers to their exit from Germany kept rising.

Both villas were now primarily rental properties. Edith had moved back to Schillerstrasse 19 to be with her mother and faithful family factotum Marie. They now live on the top floor having rented out the lower floors to their family attorney Rudi Bader and to an Alsatian doctor and his sister. More laws were passed restricting the movement of Jews and segregating them further from society. Baden-Baden, however, seems safer. It is an internationally known resort where kings and princes came to play. Here the government wanted to portray a gentler side. Wealthy visitors continue to come including an old family friend Albert T Otto, a wealthy New Yorker who often visits them. Each time he leaves they give him items to take back to Willy such as his cello and stamp collection. As host to The Olympics in 1936, Hitler does not want to give the country a bad reputation. Anti-Semitic actions are toned down. But even in idyllic Baden-Baden there were Nazi sympathizers who used the twisted legal web to trap the innocents.

Less than a month after their return Edith received a summons to appear at the main customs office. She had been denounced by her tenant Koch, a relative of the German employee of the Parisian bank named Nino Rupp, of having exchanged undeclared Reichsmarks in Paris. On the 20th of November 1934 Edith is jailed for eight days under investigative detention. For a long time, she heard nothing further.

While Edith waited in 1935, the government continued to issue restrictive laws. Klara's brother-in-law for instance could no longer import tobacco which meant his business was going bankrupt. New laws were used to strangle the regimes opponents. From the very first decree, ironically named Decree for the Protection of the People and the State, the new Nazi government was determined to eliminate the basic rights guaranteed by the constitution. Goebbels had already said that the task of National Socialism was "to erase the year 1789 from German history". Individual rights meant nothing anymore versus the state. In June of 1935 paragraph 2 of the criminal code was rewritten: "That person will be punished who commits an act which the law declares punishable, or which *deserves* punishment according to the fundamental principle of a criminal statute or *healthy popular opinion.*" The law now served the state as Hitler emphasized to his minister of justice when he said that the attorney must become "a person representing the state, like the judge". Crimes of the state were now covered by a cloak of twisted laws. The law was now used even though there was no belief in The Law. Attorneys were no longer protectors and defenders of their clients but were now another arm of the state apparatus. The Nuremburg Laws of 1935 had already removed citizenship from the Jews. They had become state property and were disenfranchised by law. The legal machinery of the law could now be used to strip away assets and the stateless citizens were disinherited.

41

On the 18th of February 1936 Edith was brought to trial for having smuggled money out of Germany which was considered a treasonous offense. She was sentenced to seven months in prison and fined 14000 Reich marks. As she wrote her brother, "You know where I will spend my birthday. It started on my last birthday when I was invited to appear at the main customs office and the year before that Mama was sick and we had to go to Palma. My life seems to be going to pieces."

After writing to her brother she decided, over the objections of her attorney, to visit the judge and ask whether an appeal could be made. The judge, who was an old family friend, advised against it as the prosecutor might increase her sentence and fine. The new legal machinery of Germany really didn't allow for an appeal. Judges had to fulfill the Fuehrer's wishes. The judge told Edith she would be sent to Gotteszell (literally God's cell) which was an old Dominican cloister founded in 1200 but turned into a prison at the time of Napoleon and today was a women's prison. Gotteszell was the first Nazi concentration camp for women political prisoners. At the time, her mother wrote to Willy that the renters told her "Edith has the sympathies of the entire town". In retrospect Klara regrets her decision to go to Paris. Although at the time many Jews who had left in 1933 returned the

following year as many thought Hitler would not remain in power. Even U.S. Ambassador Dodd notes in June of 1934 that he couldn't imagine Hitler and his cronies would last much longer as he regarded them as 16-year-old clowns.

Now that her mother is in protective custody, Edith can only imagine what will happen. In her case they desperately tried to prove that she only had Swiss francs. Her mother went to Zurich and received a letter from their Swiss bank which showed they had withdrawn the money for the trip. But the Swiss evidence was rejected. At the time Edith had written that she hoped to receive her passport after leaving prison and believed that within a few weeks after that they would be able to join Willy in New York. After her release on the 4th of October 1936, they had gone to the U.S. consulate in Stuttgart on November 6th and started the paperwork necessary for obtaining a visa. The final steps were to regain their passports and the all- important good conduct certificate. Everything seemed within their reach. Now there was uncertainty.

On April 2nd Klara returned from her investigative detention. Edith writes to Willy, "it was then that we discovered what it was all about. Where is the money that we inherited when Papa died, particularly what happened to the pound sterling and other foreign denominations since 1925 and what other foreign assets did we have either under our own names or that of others? Mama answered truthfully that you, Walter Herrmann and Dr. Siegl took care of our affairs."

"The authorities are continuing their investigation and yesterday, Wednesday the 7th of April have returned at 5:30 p.m. to take our dear mother to jail again. She is much braver than I, composed and secure in the knowledge of her innocence. An arrest warrant has not yet been issued—hopefully it won't happen --- but maybe it will happen this evening." After the Olympics of August 1936, the entire legal system of Germany was directed to extract liquid assets from enemies of the state. Klara and Edith were treated as enemies. In early February of 1936 the Gestapo had already been placed above the law with no judicial review of their activities. Edith knew they were powerless against this supra legal arm of the state. Although Edith does not know what will happen to her mother who is now in investigative detention, she still hopes to receive her passport soon. A legal cloak of cruelty is slowly enveloping their lives.

The balance of 1937 Edith works in the garden and takes care of the household. Willy has found a German, Herr Maier, who lives in New Jersey and would like to return to Germany exchanging his house in Weehauken, New Jersey for Edith's villa, Fremersbergstrasse 10. A great deal of time is spent trying to arrange the exchange. There are appointments in Karlsruhe with customs officials and with the Revenue Department to obtain permission. Herr Mayer, after staying a few days in Schillerstrasse even goes to Berlin to obtain the necessary permits. Every cent that is spent on postage, taxes, house maintenance means less for food. Edith is losing weight. In June, as a diversion, she goes to a movie theater and sees a story about Chopin, aptly named "A Farewell Waltz" (Abschiedswalzer). She finds the melody of the Nocturne haunting and writes out a line of music in a letter to her brother asking him whether he recognizes it. She is happy that Willy is playing the cello and is socially busy visiting the Hirschhorns and the Morgenthaus who are old family friends. From time to time, she even plays the piano and sings. By the end of July, she writes that "I am no longer alone as I have a new companion, a cute wireless terrier named Lumpy." A few weeks later as she returns from the market she notes to her brother," I encountered Ernst W we almost bumped into each other. He didn't think it was necessary to greet me." Other former friends cross the street so as not to pass by her. "Lumpy is really sweet and my best companion…at least with him there are no disappointments. I am now down to 100 pounds. I eat my bread with tears, there is more crying than eating. Do you think your dog Ginger will get along with Lumpy? He is so playful. I send him out alone to his girlfriend. He arrives back after half a day, dead tired but extremely playful."

Towards the end of October 67 year old Marie, their trusted household help who had to leave their employ due to new laws forbidding Aryans to work for Jews, arrives and stays with Edith for a few days. "She cleans and polishes from dawn till dusk and feels completely in her element. She is trying hard to spoil me and feeds me so that my clothes will fit again." To show her appreciation, she knits a hat and baby jacket for Marie's new niece. Marie is amazed how well Edith can cook and bake. Shortly after Marie leaves, Herr Meyer comes and explains that the authorities have forbidden the house exchange. Edith writes that "an exchange is now hopeless." She tries to keep her spirits up by knitting a sweater for her brother and teaching a young neighbor how to make decorative items with a coping saw.

In the beginning of November, she attends a concert and sends her brother a copy of the program along with a clipping of a newspaper review. "It wasn't as beautiful and phenomenal as the critic writes; the hall was half empty. The singer kept giving encores: from R. Strauss Cecilia, from Handel's Largo, etc. the accompanist was terrific, I liked him the best." She concludes, "My heart is heavy and I long to be able to see you and talk with you… If it only was already. Sometimes I doubt it will happen. I weighed myself at the drugstore…94 pounds!! Do you think I can still sing?"

Later that month, Germany quietly ramps up its plans for war. On November 5th, at the Hossbach conference which excluded most of the members of Hitler's cabinet, Hitler announces his plan to expand German lands by annexing Austria and overpowering Czechoslovakia. He sees this expansion necessary to make the German Reich more self- sufficient. He feels Germany has enough coal but covets the steel and armaments factories of Czechoslovakia. At the meeting Field Marshall von Bloomberg, General von Fritsch, and Foreign Minister von Neurath argue that these plans are too risky and should not be undertaken. (In February 1938 all three are dismissed from their posts.)

On December 25$^{th}$ Edith travels to Mannheim to visit her mother who is still in investigative detention. She visits her Aunt Helen and Uncle Albert, and they insist she stay overnight. All are worried. On her return to Baden-Baden friends bring her small gifts. "You see I haven't been completely forgotten". On the 8$^{th}$ of January 1938 her mother is released. She writes to her son, "Lately I have not been well. Edith is taking loving care of me and soon I should be ship shape. Have you been swimming and keeping up with your music? When Edith is feeling better, she will have to practice singing again."

They know that release from detention does not mean the investigation has been completed. In the meantime, an indictment has also been issued for "Dr. B.W. Herrmann presently living in Port Chester, New York." He has been indicted since he is listed as co-owner of Villa Edith and executor of his father's estate. In early March Willy receives a letter from Strasbourg, France from Bill's friend whom he does not know but who has just visited his family. He writes "Since the same proceedings are directed against you the state has taken a security mortgage on your house of RM50,000. The entire fortune of your mother has been seized and impounded including her

*Painting of Klara in 1912 by Maximillian Schultze-Strahler an artist who had been loaned money by my grandfather. When he couldn't repay, he painted portraits of the family*

furniture. For this reason, you should ask Mr. Otto to send RM1000 to attorney Roth in Rastatt noting that the money is to help support your sister. Under no circumstance should you send money directly as it would immediately be seized. Attorney Roth will write to you about your stamp collection. Your mother is accused of having sent you two albums. You should answer that these were your property since childhood. Otherwise, your mother will lose the RM50,000. In the future you should not use a return address on your envelopes addressed to your sister. Write about inconsequential things since your letters are all being censured. Don't press them about their emigration. Mr. Otto or someone else should write that your sister has offers as a secretary or household help so that she can get her passport. Your sister wants to know whether you received the package sent from Strasbourg with the silverware. If yes, then write on *my birthday I sat on a wonderfully set table.* If not, then write *on my birthday I was alone.* In this way your sister will have acknowledgement and know that you received this letter. Please give my regards to Bill and tell him that under no circumstance should he come to Germany as it may be dangerous for him."

The next letter from Edith asks, "Did you have a nicely set table for your birthday? My birthday yesterday was spent very modestly. Mama was sorry she could only give me a hyacinth plant. I told her my best gift was that she was with me again. The little boy in the house (Hermann Bader) was so cute. He kept calling for the birthday child and gave me a golden bracelet with the sentiment engraved *in eternal remembrance.* Please send him an American toy (he is 5 ½ years old). He keeps asking how Uncle Willy is doing. We are so happy your practice is busier. For your sake I hope there are many sick children." While she tries to keep her spirits up, she writes:" I just can't bring myself to sing. I am frequently in despair. The happiest amongst us is the dog." The tax inspector has visited the house and placed a seal with the eagle and swastika on every piece of furniture including the Bechstein grand piano.

*Edith at the age of 7 in 1912*

A few days after her birthday, on the 12th of March Germany annexes Austria and German soldiers march in unopposed.

As the month of April progresses Edith again writes to the authorities to ask for her passport. Meanwhile "...we have almost no money and still they won't let me leave to earn my bread. And now mother has had another attack. Her blood pressure is above 200. The doctor has withdrawn some blood and she feels better...the happiest is our dog. He leaves daily to look for a bride and sometimes brings a friend for our approval." Then in late April they receive the official summons for Willy which is also published in the newspaper. Now they know that there will be a trial on the 27th of June 1938 in Mannheim in a Special Court (Sondergericht).

Roland Freisler, Secretary of State of the Reich's Ministry of Justice called the Sondergericht "the panzer troops of justice". It was Freisler as chief jurist who helped twist the law toward Nazi goals. Special Courts were established after 1933 and consisted of three judges. There was no appeal of their decision and verdicts were immediately applied. While there was the appearance of a judicial process, defense attorneys were appointed by the state and evidence could not be called into question since the court was outside the normal judicial system. It was used against people accused of a wide variety of treasonous actions. The Nazi law was as twisted as their cross.

On May 10th Willy receives another letter from Strasbourg this time handwritten by the wife of the family barber Frau Reeb. Letters from Strasbourg are not censored and thus the writers are free to express themselves. "How are you dear doctor? Surely better than all of us here. Your mother asked me to tell you how things are which I gladly do since I am very attached to your family. There are things we cannot express in Germany... ... She asks you to read the enclosed letter carefully. Attorney Roth believes your mother will be sentenced because of negligence and hopes that the time she has spent in investigative detention will be deducted from her sentence. Your mother believes that all her assets that have been impounded will probably be appropriated by the state. Her financial support is necessary *but not by you* always by others. Please never mention this letter as your letter could be opened by the authorities and would come back to haunt us. "

"We have enjoyed the radio you sent us and the beautifully stamped envelopes you sent as my husband is such an avid collector. We are so sorry for the poor people here that have to endure so much. We don't know how they can bear it. For us, according to the times, we have had a very hard winter. We have lost many of our customers both through death and emigration. Health wise it could be better, and you know the burden of our souls."

A final letter from another family friend sent from Strasbourg notes: "Your mother is not well and suffers from stomach cramps and migraines. A few days ago, she fainted in the bathroom and damaged her nose and face. She is a bit better now......they are hoping for an amnesty from the court. My wife tells me that both your mother and sister had a very bad day. They cried all night and discussed ways of ending it all. Please help them financially. For me this is the last letter I can write since my international passport is expiring and there will be military difficulties for me if I try to leave the country."

The family still has friends in Baden who try to help but the bureaucracy remains a burden. Edith has written to the consulate in Stuttgart to ask whether they can help but they answer, "The Consulate cannot intercede with the German authorities with a view to expediting the return of your passport." She is thus caught in a legal limbo. She can't get an exit visa without her passport. Her only hope is that once the trial of her mother (and brother in absentia) is over the authorities will release her passport. She believes Willy will be fairly represented by the court appointed attorney as she writes, "I don't know your attorney personally, but I know you have been in touch with him and that he has your interest at heart." She closes by saying "even though summer has started here there seem to be few visitors in town. Today I trimmed the dog's hair, and he looks really adorable." She also tells him to thank Mr. and Mrs. Hirschorn, The Morgenthaus, John Hay and Mr. Otto for the money she has received via a bank in Berlin. The bulk of the money received went to pay new taxes that had been levied. On June 20,1938 her mother leaves for Mannheim and her court date. Due to financial constraints her daughter cannot accompany her mother.

From February of 1933 until May of 1938 there were more than 17 laws and decrees on the books regarding economic sabotage, foreign exchange transactions, treason against the German economy, and registration of Jewish assets. Taxes were also levied on Jewish emigrants. It was not a coincidence that laws banning new political parties, initiating the confiscation of the property of "enemies of the people and the state," and removing German citizenship came into effect on the same day, July 14, 1933. Accomplishing this required a close degree of cooperation between the Gestapo and the financial administration authorities.

In April 1937 Reinhard Heydrich, head of the Gestapo Central Office, issued new guidelines for denaturalization cases, in accordance with Himmler's instructions. Henceforth specific reports were to be prepared on emigrant Jews' economic activity and on any debts or unpaid taxes they had left behind. Himmler recommended moving against the Jews "with greater severity than before regarding denaturalization," even if no evidence existed of their anti-German activity abroad. He characterized currency and tax-law infringements or other crimes such as fraud, blackmail, or document falsification as examples of "typically Jewish behavior that was damaging to the people."

In May new measures were taken including Confiscation of Emigrants' Property and Preventative Measures regarding Evasion of Foreign Exchange Regulations. Hitler needs to raise as much money as he can to fund his war effort. Officially the government at this time wanted to rid Germany of its Jewish population and encouraged emigration. They were *free* to go. But what would the court command? In a few days Edith would learn the worst.

On June 27, 1938, the trial takes place in Mannheim and the next day The **Zwastika Banner** headline states *Just Punishment for Jewish Underhanded Dealings* with a subtitle of *The Judgement in the Trial of the Jewess Clara Herrmann reads: Two Years and 10 months*

*Penitentiary.* There is a large sketch of Clara with her attorney. In addition to the prison sentence fines are levied totaling RM45000 with an additional RM50000 levied against Willy in absentia. The prison sentence is reduced by 7 months for the time Clara spent in investigative detention. The next subheading reads *The Jews damage the State* and details the crimes against the sections and paragraphs of the 1933 Law on Treason against the German Economy and other sections and paragraphs of other laws. It then states that the *District Attorney in his summation explained that one would like to see the Jews emigrate, but not thereby damaging the German currency.* Since 1933, the article continues, one has repeatedly discovered that the Jews either by themselves or through middlemen have transferred their fortunes abroad. From the general diatribe against the Jews the reporter then describes the case against Clara primarily because of her Swiss bank account. The authorities already knew that this account existed since she paid her daughter's RM14000 fine from this account and indeed it was known by the Parisian bank employee who had earlier denounced them. Much is made of their trip to Paris and Mallorca. The article concludes "if there is one thing that saddens us, it is that Willi(sic) Herrmann has escaped his holiday resort in a German prison."

When Edith reads the newspaper, she quickly writes a letter to her mother trying to console her. The drawing of her mother disturbs her as it shows a hooked nose she never had, On the 30th of June Klara writes to her daughter and notes that her fate has been sealed "so terribly as I would not have believed." She tells her attorney "Now I am dead to the world." Even though she has no money or stamps, she has been given permission to write a letter. "I told attorney Roth I didn't want to see anyone anymore, but after receiving your unhappy letter I want to see you again before I leave. Come quickly and bring some money and stamps if you can. Let Marie come to help you. Take time for everything and depend on no one. Don't be sad, think of it as having been preordained. If our dear God gives me the strength, we will see each other again. And if it doesn't happen, you and Willy will know I always strove to do what is right and good." She also notes that three young women are her cellmates.

Immediately upon receipt of the letter Edith takes the train to Mannheim to visit her mother and bring her the few things she requested. Upon arrival she discovers her mother has already left. She asks the prison official where her mother has been sent and is told that she is going to the women's penitentiary in Aichach which is in upper Bavaria. They tell her that Aichach is between Augsburg and Munich. When she gets back to Baden-Baden, she writes her a long letter which she illustrates with cartoons. She tries to lift her own spirits but feels completely alone, isolated from her family, isolated by the society in which she had grown up, isolated in her own home where she now occupies what had been an attic. She realizes it is now up to her to devise her exit strategy from Germany. She doesn't want to leave without her furniture and piano even though they now all carry tags with the seal of state, the eagle and swastika.

# Aichach, Auctions and Alone

Klara left Mannheim on the 7th of July 1938 at 7:30am riding in a 3rd class compartment of an express train to Wurzburg. A young woman in the jail had given her three heavily buttered pieces of bread. It seemed with each puff of the steam engine she sighed in syncopation. As a proper Victorian woman, the widow of one of the leading men in town her world had come crashing down. She was alone in the compartment. In Wurzburg she was given something to eat and allowed to lie down for about two hours. By the time they left for Nuremburg four women had joined. They arrived in Nuremburg about 6 pm and were fed. She then slept with three other women in the room provided. The next morning, they were given coffee and another six women joined. All were given a packet with bread and a large piece of sausage. Klara writes that she was happy to be in a compartment with a woman whose status resembled hers. They arrived in Aichach around noon and Klara was pleased that she had only spent one night in transit whereas some of the women had travelled 8-14 days. A woman met them at the train station, and they were driven in a van with two benches to the penitentiary.

The women's penitentiary was built in 1904 -1908 in an architectural style reminiscent of the baroque. An octagonal central hall

which houses the administrative staff is flanked by four wings of three floors each. Every floor contains 16 – 20 cells which house 1-2 persons or some with as many as 4. A barbed wire fence surrounds the buildings with a masonry outer wall in the form of a hexagon. At every corner of the exterior walls there are watch towers with armed guards. The prison was originally built for a catholic constituency and has a church as part of the complex.

Immediately upon arrival they were provided with a baked fish and some potato salad. "Then we needed to change our clothing. I have a black dress with a blue neckerchief and a blue apron. They don't wear a hood or scarf here. The dress is a sort of alpaca and not too heavy, with a white blouse and slip. I have a bright cell with white walls and a good bed with a three- part mattress and soft white rugs on the floor. I also have a calendar on the wall. The food is ample and good, much better than it was in Karlsruhe and Mannheim. They treat us well here as long as you follow the rules….it is said that this was once a cloister, so I tell myself I am a nun." The prison doctor who examined her had noted that due to her heart condition prison staff are to raise and lower the bed for her. There is a landscaped courtyard where they may walk for an hour each day.

By the time Klara writes her first letter from prison, Edith has already written two letters to her. However, prisoners are only allowed to receive one letter every two months. The prison warden shows Klara the second letter without letting her read it. She sees her daughters handwriting and is terribly upset those rules allow a letter only every two months. "I begged the director to let me see your letter, but he wouldn't allow it saying that there was nothing special in it." Rules are printed on the prison stationary. "Visits are allowed once every three months. Money may be sent. Food may neither be sent or brought. Stories of released prisoners are not necessarily to be believed." She writes that both Edith and Willy may write a letter, but a censor has written in pencil that she may only receive one letter every two months.

Although her trials have just begun, Klara says, "I feel healthier here and thank God I don't need to worry about money and such things anymore. I don't care what people say or think about my fate. I heard what was printed in the paper and don't need to reproach myself." She closes her first letter from prison by asking Willy to do everything he can to support his sister and bring her to America.

While Klara is being transported to Aichach, a conference is taking place in Evian-les-Bains, France to discuss the Jewish refugee problem. Roosevelt had hoped that the conference would result in more countries accepting refugees. By now there were more than 1.5 million stateless Jews since Hitler's racial laws were applied not only in Germany but also in Austria. America's agreement to accept 30,000 refugees was a paltry sum in view of the magnitude of the problem. Only two countries agreed to accept refugees: The Dominican Republic and later Costa Rica. Willy had gone to Santo Domingo first where he was welcomed by President Trujillo who wanted to

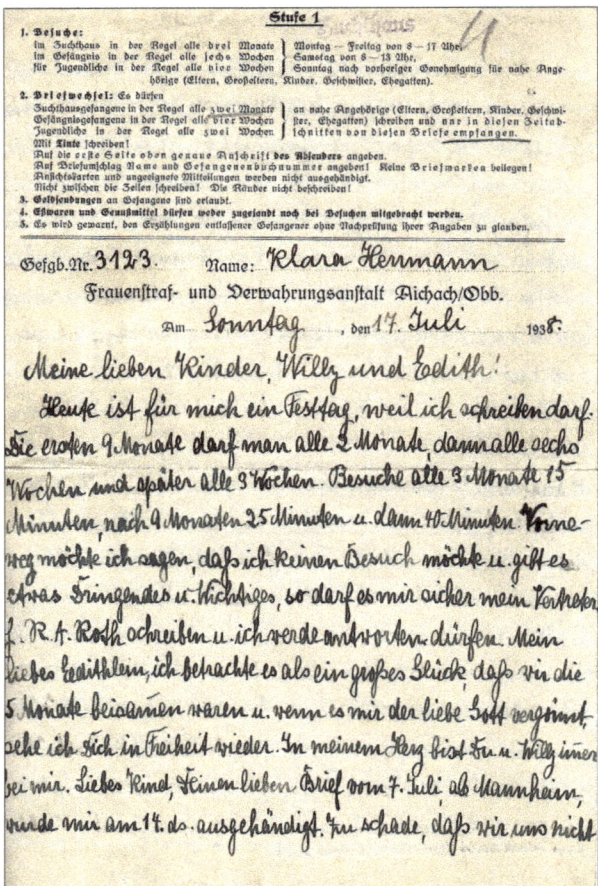

raise the education level of the islanders and hoped professionals like doctors and teachers would help him reach his goal. Willy loved the climate and the welcome reception but contracted malaria. Because of his health he then left for America where he passed the New York State boards test for medical doctors.

While Edith is alone, she is not forsaken. Although her mother's sisters have not visited since her mother was in investigative detention, there are still local friends who try to help. In mid- August little Gerhilde, the five-year-old daughter of their former seamstress Frau

Haas, comes and spends a week with her so she isn't totally alone. Gerhilde frequently walks Lumpy as that seems to be a safe alternative to letting him run free. By now Edith is afraid to walk alone on the street. Whenever she receives monies from the States (from friends of her brother) she rushes to pay doctor bills or maintenance costs with little left over for herself. Her attorney continues efforts to get her external passport released. The authorities are now auctioning items in her villa on Fremersbergstrasse 10 and items belonging to her mother. She writes to her brother, "You know me. I am courageous and continue to fight. But sometimes I am overcome with thoughts of suicide. Then I think of mother and you and hope we all three will

be together again. Next Monday Christine my former household help will come for a deposition and testify that the furniture here was in my house and belongs to me."

Her mother's letter at the end of August notes with sadness that she was called to the director's office. He briefly shows her a ten- page letter from Edith which of course she was not allowed to read. She may only receive a one- page letter that may be written on both sides of the paper. By this time all her letters are being controlled by censors as can be seen from the back of her envelopes. She shares her cell with another Jewish woman her age and in the evening, they play cards together. She is knitting socks which she enjoys. Their evening meal was noodle soup with bacon and a cucumber salad.

It is September now with the machinery of war rumbling louder. There are several meetings of Hitler and Neville Chamberlain where Hitler declares his desire to annex parts of Czechoslovakia. He states that it is the last claim which he will make in Europe and Chamberlain believes him and says he is a man whose word can be relied upon. After his second meeting that month Chamberlain comes back to Britain and declares that there will be peace in our time. Shortly thereafter on October 1st German forces occupy Sudetenland.

By mid- September Edith watches in horror as her mother's furniture, including some of hers, is taken away along with her clothing, linens, porcelain (including a collection of Meissen figurines), silver and jewelry. The clothing and shoes that were seized included the new items she and her mother had purchased for their planned trip to America. The excitement causes Edith to vomit repeatedly. There are times she writes that she only has enough money to eat four days a week. Often, she has less than RM15 at her disposal describing herself as destitute. Whenever she receives money, she hurries to pay taxes so that more won't be taken from her. Doctor, dentist, and attorney bills are mounting. She writes that Christine testifies under oath that the furniture remaining in the Schillerstrasse attic living quarters belong to Edith and were in her former house.

"I can't express how upset I am that they have impounded your furniture and piano," her mother writes from Aichach. "You must fight for your rights. Decorator Egl and Christine will surely testify on your behalf......In a few days it will be the anniversary of Papa's death and I can't visit the cemetery. I have two prayer books and will pray for him. If he were still with us, we would have been protected from all this. Yesterday a rabbi was here. I did not want to speak with him. The warden told me today that he was very disappointed that he couldn't

*This piece of furniture had Nazi seals on it and Edith was initially barred from moving it.*

*The Italian renaissance bench also had Nazi seals on it.*

speak to me. What good is all this comfort? There are neither holidays nor feast days for me now." Klara is not the only one to feel isolated.

Edith alone in the attic of the house where she spent so many beautiful hours needed to find activities to keep her from desperation. She has a coping saw and makes gifts for friends with scrap pieces of wood which she then decorates. Occasionally she plays the piano. Her favorite piece is a song from the last movie she had seen, when it was still safe to see movies, the film *A Farewell Waltz*. It was about the life of Chopin and two women who had loved him. Immediately after seeing the film, she had bought the sheet music with the song *In mir klingt ein Lied* (There is a song in my heart). She wrote her brother about the film and asked whether he knew the melody telling him occasionally she forced herself to play the piano. The music was based on Chopin's Opus 10, number 3 etude which Chopin himself had said was the most beautiful melody he had ever written. It was both beautiful and melancholy. Edith began to play the piano and sing:

There is a song in my heart
A little song

In which a dream of silent love unfolds…

For you alone

An ardent unfulfilled desire wrote this melody…Do you hear the music,

The tender music?

How she wished that there might be a song in her heart. Darkness was descending. It was difficult for her to sing. Music had always been an important part of the family's life. There was a sunny room downstairs that had been the music room where the grand piano had been. There they often played music with her mother accompanying her on the piano while her brother played the cello. Many well-known musicians had been their guests. She remembered the Friedberg/ Flesch/Becker trio playing in their music room when she was a teenager. It was so much fun to listen to their stories of encounters with Schumann and Brahms. As she paged through her autograph book, she came across the picture and signature of Leo Blech the well-known composer and conductor. The year he visited them he was preparing to conduct the premiere of Die Frau Ohne Schatten by Richard Strauss. She and her brother would often play games whistling or singing motifs from Wagner operas and the other had to guess which opera it was. Before her mother was imprisoned, she sometimes signed her letters with a treble clef and e note followed by "dith" thus spelling her name musically.

Everyone told her to leave Germany. Her brother was waiting in America. Her friends couldn't understand why she hadn't left. She couldn't leave without her passport. And even if she had it, she didn't want to leave her mother in prison. Her Kafkaesque condition continued to suppress her spirits. Arthur Schnitzler, an Austrian physician and author, had written in her autograph book when he visited them in August of 1923, "As long as one is young all doors are open; behind each door the world begins" from his play the Lonely Way. Right now, all the doors were shut, and she was on her own lonely way.

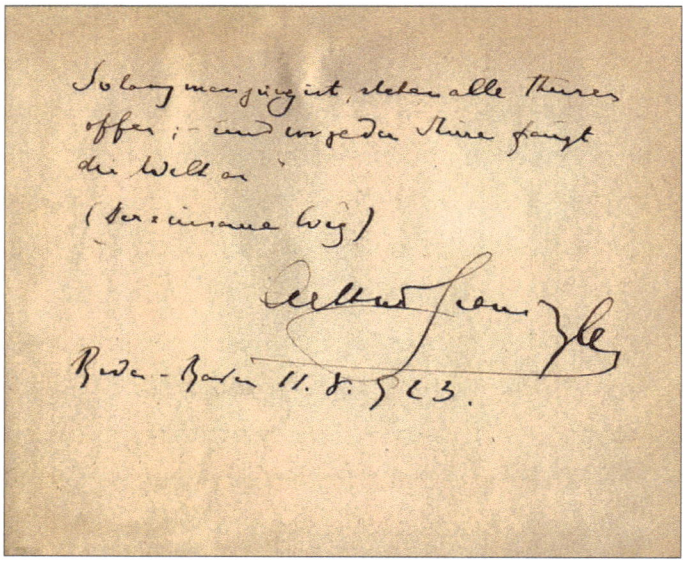

To while away the time, Edith studies a series of 13 genealogy tables which were sent to her mother in 1936 while she was in Gotteszell. They were prepared by Albert Teutsch, a distant cousin, who was a lawyer in nearby Karlsruhe. After he was forbidden to practice law, he turned his energies toward producing genealogy tables. My mother also believed that it was one way to counter Hitler's red books by which Germans in public offices proved their Aryan descent. The genealogy tables proved that her family had lived in Germany for centuries. The Teutsch family was easily traced back to 1590 to Gershon Aschkenazy. The word Ashkenazy means German in medieval Hebrew. Later ancestors dropped the Hebrew word Aschkenazy and replaced it with Teutsch, which was probably the Yiddish way of saying Deutsch.

Every year at Passover Edith had been reminded of the exodus and expulsion of Jews from Egypt. While she certainly was aware of strains of antisemitism in Germany her family had tried hard to assimilate. She was the first Jewish student at the private girls' high school which was under the patronage of the Grand Duchess of Baden. Each year she remembered curtseying when the Grand Duchess came to the school. Her father was eager to assimilate. They naturally thought they were German. Even though they had had their citizenship denied by decree, the document before her proved that her earliest ancestors arrived in the Rhine River valley from Italy sometime between the 9th and 10th century.

Edith is aware of both past and current events. Reading the newspapers increases her feeling of dread. She and her mother have now missed three appointments with the U.S. Consul in Stuttgart to obtain their visas. In her existential isolation, there seems to be no exit. As she had written in an earlier letter to the consul in Stuttgart, "I have in my quality of Jewess nothing to expect or seek in the 3rd Reich." The net of Nazi laws and fines immobilize her, things her brother in America does not understand. In early October of 1938 she writes, "In my apartment up here every piece has a collateral security seal. I can't dispose of my house without the permission of the authorities and as a result can- not raise money by either obtaining a mortgage or selling a single item I possess. The entire fortune of Mama has been confiscated. I don't qualify for public assistance since none of our houses have a mortgage." Although her brother, through friends, sends her small sums whenever he can, she does not realize that his new practice is also in poor financial condition. The depression is keenly felt in America and many of his patients are unable to pay. In an affidavit supporting his sister's immigration he notes that his monthly income is $150.

Early in October, after a meeting with Heinrich Rothmund Head of the Swiss Police, Germany agrees to stamp a large red J in passports belonging to Jews. After the meeting they decided to add another identifier by having women use the name Sarah and men Israel. This was to go into effect in the new year.

By the end of October Edith's prospects improve. Through the efforts of her attorney the customs office in Karlsruhe will release her external passport which is no longer required as security. She can obtain her passport once she shows the authorities that she has a letter confirming an appointment with the U.S. consul. At the same time, she receives the following notice from the financial authorities:

> *With the conclusion of this settlement there are no longer differences of opinion between the Department of Finance and Edith Herrmann which relate to the debtor Mrs. Klara Herrmann. It is acknowledged that the items in the apartment of Miss Edith Herrmann are her property. The security seals may be removed except from the grand piano.*
>
> *You are free to dispose of the items in Schillerstrasse 19 —except for the grand piano. You may remove the seals yourself.*
>
> *Signed by the tax inspector Schaubeck.*

Edith is overjoyed and writes to her brother that she believes she will be able to leave in 4-6 weeks. She has asked the movers to come to measure the size of the container they will need to accommodate her furniture. They have quoted that the move will cost RM2000, so she begs her brother to have the money sent. Meanwhile her mother writes all sorts of advice to her on items she could pawn or sell to raise money recognizing that she is not eating enough and that her daughter's health is deteriorating. Every financial step that is taken requires permission from the authorities. Money may only be raised to pay Aryan vendors. When the first-floor tenant, Dr. Krauss, terminates his lease she is given permission to sell a large mirror, a lamp in the form of a grape from the veranda, an electric sconce, and a six-armed brass candelabra in order to pay doctor bills.

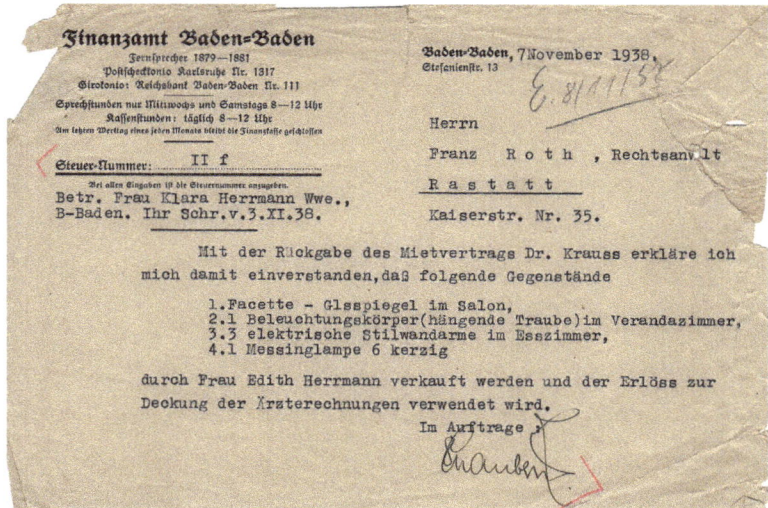

On November 8, 1938, Edith receives permission to move from the currency control department in Karlsruhe. She believes that she will be able to obtain her visa quickly and that she can depart from Hamburg on the 16th of November realizing that it all depends on the visa. She has asked Marie to come to help her pack. That afternoon she gets an unexpected visitor with ominous news. It is Rudi Bader the attorney who has been handling the rental agreements with her tenants and who is himself a tenant in Schillerstrasse. She often takes care of his little boy Hermann, called Manny, while his parents have parties or are away. Edith has already written that Lumpy, her wirehaired terrier, and Manny are her two most faithful companions. From her attic vantage point, she also observed many Nazi officials, some in uniform, attend Bader's parties.

Rudi pleads with Edith to leave Germany as quickly as possible. He tells her that a pogrom has been planned for the next evening and that Jewish properties will be attacked. However, he has a plan to protect Schillerstrasse and Edith from harm. He will hang a large Nazi banner from the upstairs window and assures her that no harm will come to her or the house. Rudi is close to tears. If he had known, he says, he would never have joined the party. Rudi can't exit the party. For the next few days Edith can't exit the house.

Because the SS did not want to bother the hotel guests still in Baden-Baden, the night of November 9, 1938, was quiet. In order to execute the pogrom, they also needed SS reinforcement from other communities who were occupied that evening. On November 10 the serenity of the splendid spa was shattered. By all accounts the viciousness and the brutality of the attacks exceeded those in most of the other parts of Germany. Early that morning all Jewish men above the age of 18 are gathered and brought to the police station. Then they are marched through the town and taken to the synagogue. The steps leading up to the house of worship are lined with a gauntlet of both uniformed and civilian men cursing, threatening, and spitting. Prayer shawls are placed on the steps forcing the men to step on them as they mounted the stairs. By the time the men entered the synagogue the interior was already desecrated. They were forced to remove their hats. A former high school professor under duress had to read a passage from *Mein Kampf* while standing on the elevated platform used as a pulpit. Then all had to sing the Nazi anthem, the Horst-Wessel song. Those men who had to go to the bathroom were forced to relieve themselves against the wall of the synagogue while being beaten. On the women's balcony SS men were seen preparing a fire. The men were then marched across the street to the Central Hotel where lunch was hastily organized.

*Oil painting of Willy in 1912*

As the men were eating lunch, cantor Gruenfeld came in to announce that the synagogue was in flames. Buses were waiting to transport the men to the train station. All men between the ages of 18 and 60 were loaded onto the buses. The train took them via Karlsruhe and Stuttgart to Dachau where they were imprisoned for a month before returning to Baden-Baden. Upon their return they discovered that the Nazis were now demanding that they pay RM9000 to have the ruins demolished. Additional atonement taxes are levied to have the Jews pay for the rain of ruins on the 9th and 10th.

Rudi's plan to protect the house using the Nazi banner as shield was effective but Edith is devastated when she hears that the synagogue has been destroyed. Her father and uncle had been major fundraisers and driving forces to have their house of worship built. The architect they chose designed a building in a neo-Romanesque style with two towers that reminded some of the churches in Speyer, Worms and Mainz which had been the center of Jewish German life for a thousand years. Architecturally it reminded viewers of the assimilation of Jews in Germany. At the dedication of the building in August of 1899 there was a representative of the Grand Duke of Baden as well as other functionaries. Both Edith's uncle, Ernst Herrmann who was an attorney, and her father, Carl Theodore Herrmann, are speakers at the celebration dinner that evening. They speak not only about their love for the new building, but also for their love of the Fatherland. It was good she thought that both had died before this desecration. She was now more determined to leave as soon as possible and writes "I am sure I will get my visa this week. The packers are coming on the 14th, and I would like to leave on the 23rd with the SS President Roosevelt." The smoldering synagogue snuffed out all hopes for the future. The ashes of the synagogue may be dispersed but she had the foresight to dig up the urn with her father's ashes from his gravesite. They too would go to the new world.

On the 16$^{th}$ a family friend writes to Willy from Strasbourg," Miss Edith asked me to send you a telegram but since I haven't the money, I write this letter to you. Your sister still does not have the appointment letter from the consul. Everything is packed but your sister was only able to save the few things in her apartment as all the rest has been taken away. Send a thousand marks so she can pay the mover." Following this Edith receives a letter from the family friend Albert Otto that he has been told that due to his advanced age the authorities in the states will not allow him to act as her guarantor. In her mother's bimonthly letter, she writes of her concern and worries about Edith. Does she have enough to eat? Can she manage carrying the great burdens she faces? Advice on how to pawn her jewelry and other objects of value. She has written to attorney Roth and asked him for a list of everything that had been auctioned off. "My cell mate is a proper woman who finds herself in a situation like mine. We comfort each other. The food here is not bad. If my health holds up, my greatest wish is to be reunited with my children." She is concerned whether there will be any money left for her and whether she will be able to live in Schillerstrasse when she is released pending receipt of her visa and passport. For the moment she is insulated from the vicissitudes of the outside world. On the 28$^{th}$ of November Hitler passes laws that forbid Jews from attending theaters, concerts, and cinemas.

In desperation Edith takes a train to Stuttgart on December 1 to see whether she can get her visa personally since there have been no responses to her mailed entreaties. She arrives at 10 am but is unable to even talk to anyone at the information desk until 2pm. "At 2pm there were so many people there that the staircase was filled extending into the street. When I showed them my appointment letter of the 27th of January 1937, they immediately let me in and because I only spoke English, they were especially nice to me. They retrieved my dossier and the gentleman said to me: *In the next days you will receive a reply as one of our officers is immediately working on your case.* Despite the huge crowd the gentleman escorted me to the door." She returns home where she now sleeps on a sofa and is living out of a suitcase. Her passport is at the Gestapo offices waiting for a confirmation letter from the U.S. consul.

There is no news from the consulate the following week. Everything she does requires permission from one official or another. All the running around has made her lose more weight and she writes "I've become a telegraph pole. I sold all the items I couldn't pack and in doing so discovered sales talents I didn't know I had. I must say that everyone who came was very sweet to me. You won't believe how many there were even though I didn't advertise or tell friends. Many who came –who were complete strangers to me—brought me flowers and precious gifts. They all liked dealing with me. I was happy when I could finally say Sold Out. With every piece I sold a bit of my heart went with it." She has also sold two of Willy's celli one of which was a half size Guarneri. Her sale netted RM1000. In addition, she receives RM500 for her father's marble grave monument and sells the cemetery plot for another RM200. She has raised enough to pay for her ticket to America including the ticket for her dog. Unable to pay the RM8,200 Jewish asset tax she obtains a" forced mortgage" on her Fremersberg house which she still hopes to sell for its taxed value.

By mid-December she has received permission from customs officials to send the large container and two crates to Hamburg for shipment to the states. This lifts her spirits, and she is happy that her belongings will soon be "swimming" to America. She has also been granted special permission to visit her mother on her birthday the 25th of December. She will be allowed to visit for 40 minutes without any bars separating them. In the meantime, she has pawned her jewelry for RM1383 and asks her brother to send money directly to the pawnbroker so that the ticket may be redeemed before she leaves. She sets aside RM200 from the proceeds, to be given to her mother when she is released.

Her mother was overjoyed to see her, but the minutes passed quickly, and each was left to their fate. On January 15, 1939, her mother writes an extra letter, the first time her name is written as Sarah Klara Herrmann. In it she writes of receiving a list detailing the proceeds of her furniture auction from the court in Mannheim and realizes that some of the items that had been in storage belonged to Edith. When they moved upstairs, they had stored furniture from both villas and her name was on the contract. But it is too late for Edith to correct this. Klara worries about her daughter. She admonishes her to" be careful on the street and in trams. A wrong word spoken can cause trouble."

The New Year arrives with no word from the consulate. There has also been a mix-up. Her brother sent the necessary affidavits and documents directly to the consulate instead of to her. No one knows what has happened to the papers. There are more than 8 weeks of unopened mail piled up at the consulate. The delay means that she must revisit several German officials to get an extension of her permission to leave. After much running around she receives her passport on the 9th of January.

January 1939 proves to be a cruel month. Edith takes three separate trips to the consulate with no success. A friend advised her, if she could afford to, to stay in a hotel in Stuttgart until she receives her visa. U.S. Congressman O'Day personally intervenes and cables Consul Honaker. The last week of the month she stays in the cheapest hotel and repeatedly visits the consulate. When she shows the congressman's cable she is told even if President Roosevelt had intervened nothing can happen until all the papers are in order. By the end of the month, they have found the documents, but they must now be examined to be sure they are genuine. As she leaves the hears an officer say, "Don't waste so much time with her." Her nerves are completely shot by now and she writes "I have had it. There is nothing left. I need to end it all."

In Aichach her mother is being forced to relinquish any future use of her home on Schillerstrasse. She must sign a document relinquishing her "Nutzniesungsrecht" as this, she is told, will bring RM30000 more when the forced sale of the house is completed. If she doesn't sign, then she will be liable for taxes and a further fine. She is also forbidden to contact her attorney which is a moot point since she has no more funds. "They have taken my reputation, my fortune, all my things, added this harsh penalty here and still they do not leave me in peace." For the moment she refuses to sign the document. She has also received a letter from attorney Bader that the rental income on Schillerstrasse is not sufficient to cover the costs of the maintenance and taxes. Despite these deprivations, Klara is happy that Edith now has her passport. She wishes that both her children find compatible spouses in their new world. Again, she asks her daughter whether she could redeem the pawned jewelry unaware that a law was passed that requires Jews to hand in all gold, silver and precious stones. The preceding month new laws and decrees were issued concerning the seizure of Jewish assets.

After receiving a telegram from her brother Edith goes to Stuttgart again on February 4th and again the visa is not ready. She returns bereft to her bare apartment furnished only with a sofa and suitcase. A few days later her visa is issued, and Edith is overjoyed. On Sunday February 12th she leaves Baden-Baden in the afternoon with her dog Lumpy and Hansel her canary. In the morning she says goodbye to her tenants. All of them wish her the best including Rudi who had helped her overcome all her difficulties. Her seamstress, Frau Haas, along with her daughter Gerhilde and the children of Cantor Gruenfeld accompany her to the train station. That evening she stays overnight with her Aunt Helene, Uncle Albert, and her cousins in Mannheim. The next morning, she says farewell to her Aunt Alice whose children will leave for Chicago at the end of February. At 11am Edith takes a train to Hamburg where she stays overnight with a family friend. The next day on February 14th at 5:30 in the afternoon a bus takes her and the other passengers from the offices of the United States Lines to the pier and the S.S. President Roosevelt. By the time she leaves she is down to 94 pounds. She battled the bureaucracy and has taken every scrap of her belongings with the exception of her piano. The crossing is quite stormy with winds up to 11 Beaufort scale. Edith, her dog and canary finally arrive in New York on February 26 where she is joyously greeted by her brother.

Edith is full of energy and quickly starts to earn her keep. She helps Willy in his practice; earns money by selling craft items she makes including an embroidered altar piece for a local catholic church, establishes a pension using the extra rooms they have in Port Chester, becomes a nanny which helps her to speak American English rather than the British she learned. Although she was never much interested in parties, she enjoys visiting with old family friends like Albert Otto and the Hirshorns in nearby Connecticut. As Willy writes:" In the short time that Edith is here she has become very popular. Our furniture is admired by visitors and makes it feel like a bit of Baden-Baden. A number of our former compatriots are here including Rudi Nachmann, Ernst Wolff, Mrs. Furst and her daughter, and Dr. Kuhn who has just arrived via Argentina."

In early March Edith writes to her mother in Aichach describing her journey and answering her questions. She explains that even if she could have recovered the jewelry that was pawned it would have been useless as the Germans required all Jewish gold, silver and precious stones to be turned in to the Reichsbank. "Don't worry about the jewelry we can survive without it." Her attorney in Germany believes that Klara will be able to stay in Villa Edith after she is released and for the moment need not sign the declaration requested. "In order to pay the Jewish asset tax of RM 8,200 I have given them a lien on my house. I also gave a similar lien to our attorney to compensate him. Since this is considered a forced mortgage, he effectively becomes the manager of my property." She is also happy that her furniture and crates were packed before the new laws came into effect regarding ornamental silver.

In her mother's bimonthly letter from the penitentiary on March 26 she tells them "I am alone again as the woman I shared the cell with left last month. She was pleasant. The Deutsche Bank notified me of RM438 which was credited to my account. I told them to send it to attorney Roth. I also wrote him that in the last few years I paid him well including the RM2500 which he received shortly before my trial. But I noted that during my entire hearing he never uttered a word in my defense. At the summation he only talked about the court documents. Not once did he counter the courts claims." She does not understand the changed rules of the Nazi judicial system. "Dear Edith, I have waited till you left Germany to write about my disappointment, as it has gnawed on me this entire time. My penmanship is bad. Time passes. You don't need to do anything for me."

On April 6 Klara is taken to the prison offices and given a report from the Special Court in Mannheim regarding her fines. They have been paid from the proceeds of the sale of her stocks and bonds. The sum that was left over was used to pay a part of Willy's fines with her pro forma permission.

In her early May reply Edith says, "Dear mother, don't get upset with reproaches against your attorney and don't make your burden more difficult. You have no idea how hard the lot of our coreligionists has become since the horrible deed of that unhappy youth in Paris. (This is a reference to Herschel Grynszpan who shot Ernst vom Rath a German diplomat.) Don't look to the future with bitterness but rather with hope. We will do everything we can to bring you here as soon as possible." She goes on to describe their house in detail. When she arrived, her brother's medical practice had not been busy but through her work as a nanny she has been able to refer several new patients. In answer to her mother's questions, she explains that cantor Gruenfeld's children had been very attentive to her in the weeks before her emigration and that they have been taken by Kindertransport to Great Britain while their parents are now in Switzerland. The family seamstress and her children were particularly kind. She closes by reminding her mother to "keep your head high."

Keeping Klara's head high was challenging even to Klara. In Early July she is again taken to the prison warden. He tells her that notices have been received from the city treasurer's office of Baden-Baden, the local notary and court that because of her high tax arrears she is liable to be imprisoned. In order to come up with a plan for distribution of her assets she is ordered to appear in court on July 14. The warden explains that even without her permission the house will be sold at auction. A form has been prepared that she must sign in which she refuses her right of tenancy (Nutzniesungsrecht) in Schillerstrasse. She is also shown a small package sent to her from Port Chester with a bar of Lux and a bar of Palmolive soap and a washcloth. The warden reminds her that such packages are forbidden. Meanwhile her children have appealed to the authorities for clemency, an appeal which is denied. Klara, at her children's urging, has written to Stuttgart for a visa. She receives a quick reply and is asked to appear at the consulate on September 14 which of course she is unable to do.

On September 1st Germany invades Poland. Toward the end of the month Klara has increasing headaches, vision problems and faints. She asks to see the prison doctor. He examines her and inspects her vision. The doctor recommends she see an ophthalmologist and the next morning she is accompanied by a young woman to see a doctor in Augsburg. As they walk from the train station in Augsburg, she passes a Dr. Hauser from Baden-Baden who is astonished to see her. Dr. Goetz, the ophthalmologist, spends about an hour examining her. He determines age related problems with her retina and a small cataract. She receives a prescription for both far and close vision. She is required to use eye drops for the next four weeks every morning and evening and is given medication for her blood pressure. In the month following she has another Augsburg appointment. An extra letter is allowed so that she can notify her children of her condition. "I am so glad you left me some money which I was able to use to buy my new glasses. Life and death are close to each other, and I am not so young anymore." According to prison records at 5:15am on

September 30th she rang a bell and said she couldn't take it anymore. For safety's sake they bring her to the sick bay for observation. For the next few months there are problems with mail deliveries. Records show that letters written to her children and to her attorney were censored and never sent.

In her letter of January 14th, she noted that she hasn't had a letter since August but ascribes the mail irregularities to the times. After having fainted in her cell she had asked for a cellmate and "I am now together with a very pleasant woman who is my age and a coreligionist…We have had snow here for a month. Christmas festivities were very nice and each of us received a small gift, and we had an extra fine meal. Don't worry about me. My spirits are good and so is my appetite." She looks forward to her release in September and is primarily worried about whether she will have any funds at her disposal.

In late January Oswiecim (Auschwitz) Poland is chosen by the Nazis as a site of a new concentration camp. Its purpose initially was to provide laborers for the I.G. Farben factory. The following month the first German Jews are deported into occupied Poland.

The mail gets through sporadically. Klara receives a letter from Port Chester that was sent on the 18th of October on February 14th. Her cellmate provides all sorts of recipes and cooking tips which Klara is anxious to try after her release. She is not sure she wants to see her family in Mannheim or go to Baden-Baden. Her plan is to go to Stuttgart to obtain her visa. She has heard of a charity in Berlin that provides an advance for people who need funds before emigrating. By the time she writes her next letter, Germany has already invaded Denmark, Norway, and the Netherlands. On April 16th she has signed the dissolution papers for Schillerstrasse 19. Immediately thereafter she receives a notice from the finance department's Herr Schaubek that there are no more barriers to her emigration. The police office in Baden writes that she will receive her passport depending on certification from the emigration office and the public worship office in Karlsruhe. She writes to the authorities immediately. "I know there will still be more paperwork. But the most important thing is that they will give me my freedom. God willing that the conditions in the outside world remain so that we will have the possibility to be together again." She intends to write her September letter from Stuttgart after she is freed.

By the time she writes her July 21st letter, "conditions in the outside world" have changed markedly. Belgium has surrendered, and France has been overrun and signed an armistice agreement. British forces have been evacuated from Dunkirk. The air battle for Britain has begun. War is raging on the continent. Never-the-less Klara is optimistic that she will be able to rejoin her children in America. She has secured the necessary performance bond from the emergency aid societies in both Karlsruhe and Berlin. Although she hasn't had a letter from America in four months she continues to plan for her exodus from Germany. She does not want to return to Baden-Baden, but would like to see Frau Haas, the family's seamstress, and her beloved Marie before she leaves. On the way to Hamburg, she is planning to visit her parent's grave in Mannheim and see her sister Helene and her brother-in-law Albert. "Today there are only 86(sic) days left." Klara is unaware of a series of letters between the state's attorney in Mannheim and the prison director. According to the states attorney she must serve an additional 4 days due to a residual amount of unpaid taxes of RM2000. The 4 days are calculated as being worth RM500 per day. The director writes back that according to their information the fines were paid. On July

29th the states attorney writes that some other items had been sold for RM58 bringing the arrears to RM1990. Three additional days of confinement are required in the civil prison in Aichach.

At the beginning of August, a form is sent to the Gestapo in Karlsruhe advising them of the release of a political prisoner. After providing details of the verdict and punishment there is a section in which the prison officials must describe the conduct of the prisoner. This is what is written:

> *The conduct of the prisoner while she was here, was without fault. She was courteous and quiet. Her industriousness was above average and her output considerable. The prisoner does not feel guilty and glosses over her deeds. As a genuine representative of her race, she presents herself as friendly and harmless, while she of course in reality holds national socialist Germany responsible for her deeds. She will not be active politically. She has neither the initiative nor energy for that. The prisoner directs all her thoughts to being reunited with her children in America.*

On September 1st, 1940, a cousin of Klara's, Albert Marx, is transported from a Healing and Care Institution (Heil u. Pflegeanstalt) in Giesen to Brandenburg a d Heuvel to the National Care Institute which was a euphemism for a euthanasia killing center. Albert dies in one of the early trials of the gas chambers. There Hitler's T-4 department was charged with developing the mechanics necessary for mass killings. In the beginning carbon monoxide was used but it was deemed too slow. It took another year before Bayer developed cyclone B (hydrogen cyanide) which was a much quicker process.

On the 19th of August 1940 the prison receives a letter from the Gestapo. Officials are to tell Klara that she must register with the

Gestapo in Karlsruhe upon her release. On August 26th Klara acknowledges that she must register with the Gestapo's Department II B 4. On September 4th prison authorities send three passport photos, a physical description of Klara along with two copies of her biography to the police director in Baden-Baden. On the 21st of September she receives her passport stamped with the red capital J. In the meantime, prison officials have written

to the local police asking them to pick-up their prisoner at 6:00pm on September 27, 1940. There is no record of Klara's feelings as she was freed from the women's penitentiary and reincarcerated in the court prison of Aichach. Her exodus was interrupted again.

On October 1, 1940, Klara arrives in Karlsruhe. Her sister Helene greets her on the train platform and gives her a little bit of pocket money. The Jewish aid society had informed her sister of her arrival. For the first week she is lodged in the Hotel Nassuer Hof, lodgings paid for by the Israeli community of Baden-Baden. A week later she moves to a B&B run by two elderly sisters where breakfast and a light dinner are included. "The people here are very sweet and attentive. I go to the charity kitchen for lunch and then sit outside enjoying the greenery. The papers are not yet ready at the consulate, and I worry since I haven't had a letter from you since March 11. I thank God that I am finally here. Herr Lieblich (the owner of the Central Hotel opposite the burned-out synagogue) visited me and told me that none of my old acquaintances are left in Baden. During the high holidays I attended service both days here in the house. Dear Edith, I am unable to get funds out of your accounts which have been frozen. I turned to Herr Schaubeck who had promised me assistance, but he has not responded." What Klara doesn't know is that all assets of those who emigrate are seized after their departure.

She writes one more letter from Karlsruhe on October 14th in which she mentions that form 633 has not yet been received by the consulate in Stuttgart. She has also had a visit from Marie who worked for them for almost 30 years. What she couldn't know was that in less than a week, after less than three weeks of freedom, she would lose her liberty again.

The Gauleiter of Baden, Robert Heinrich Wagner was terribly anxious to rid the area of Jews. He had been in touch with Adolph Eichmann, and they devised a plan of transport using regular coaches sending their cargo through occupied France and through Vichy France to a temporary holding camp at the foot of the Pyrenees near a town called Gurs. It was thought of as a holding camp until the extermination centers in Poland were ready. It has also been suggested that Eichmann wanted to test the reaction of the Western powers to his special Jewish transports. On the 22nd of October 1940 Klara was given a few minutes notice by a uniformed policeman to proceed to the Karlsruhe train station. She was to take her only suitcase with the belongings she had in Aichach. There were seven trains with 6,538 people from Baden-Wurttemburg and another train with 1125 from

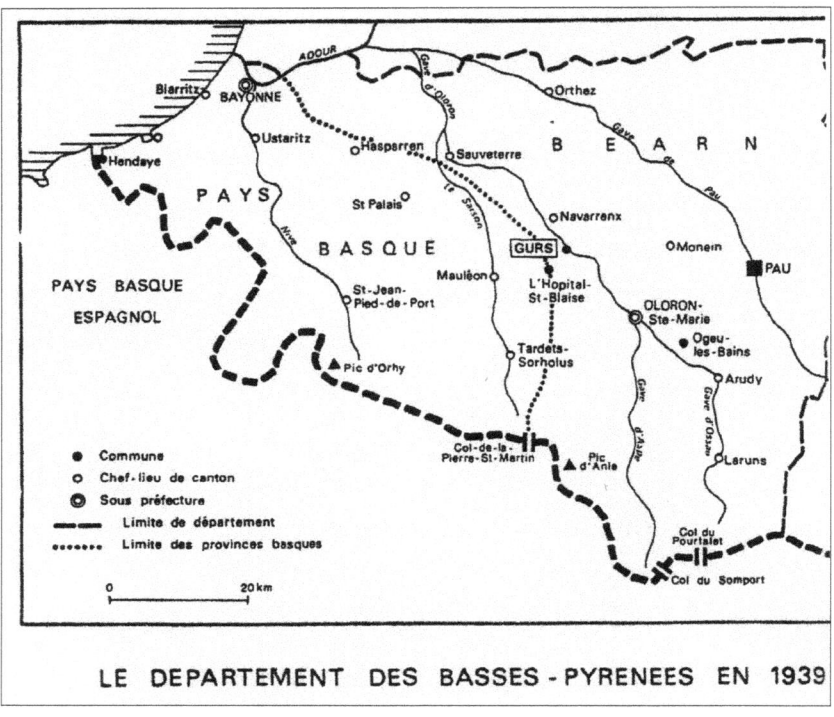

LE DEPARTEMENT DES BASSES - PYRENEES EN 1939

the Palatinate including the town of Venningen. Klara's sister Helene and brother-in-law Albert are on one of the trains. There are at least 37 Teutsch descendants among the huddled and frightened mass of passengers. Eichmann himself is in the cab of the first locomotive as it enters France. As the trains depart, Wagner reports to Berlin that Baden is the first to be rid of Jews. Somewhere en route to Gurs, Klara buys a small notebook and some onion skin paper. It takes the trains 48 hours to reach Oloron-Sainte-Marie ten kilometers from Gurs.

# Gurs

The Camp de Gurs was hastily constructed in March and April 1939 to house the Republicans fleeing the Spanish Civil War. It was never meant to be an all-seasons camp. There were 382 barracks which measured 24 meters long by 6 meters wide and 2.5 meters in height. It was a modified A frame. A flimsy tar paper was attached to a wood substrate and served as a roof covering since the camp was designed for warm weather. There was no electricity in the barracks. After it became apparent that some of the Spanish refugees would stay longer, electricity was installed, and each structure had two or three light bulbs. These types of barracks were originally used by the French in World War I to temporarily house troops before going to the trenches. The interior is completely bare. There are 13 ilots (islands) labeled A -M. Ten of the ilots have 26 barracks each while two are slightly smaller. The camp is situated along highway RN635 on swampy terrain. When it rains the area turns into mud. It is roughly 2km long by 400 meters wide. The perimeter of the camp is surrounded by two barbed wire fences eight feet high and about fifteen feet apart. French gendarmes patrol between the fences and an additional dozen watchtowers have guards at night.

The train carrying Klara took a little over two days travelling via Lyon, Dijon, Sete and Narbonne arriving at Oloron-Sainte-Marie shortly after midnight in the early morning of October 25, 1940. It is cold and rainy. She climbs aboard a truck, clutching her suitcase, for the 10- kilometer ride to Gurs. She arrives with only the clothing on her back. Drenched, cold and tired she walks through ankle deep mud and arrives at barrack 3 in ilot K. There are no mattresses or bedding, there is no food, there are no benches, there is no heat. The tired, disinherited, and dejected refugees try to sleep leaning against their few worldly possessions. Sixty to seventy-five people are cramped in the cardboard covered quarters. There is no insulation against the wind which whips down the slopes of the Pyrenees. A few days later, Klara writes "Since Thursday I am in this barrack. There are 59 of us, part of an immense mass of people. We are about 950 meters above sea level and not too distant from a town called Bo (sic). Very cold, hungry, and not heated. Too bad the emigration didn't work out. I am in greatest need, send me money, a warm coat, a dress, a slip,

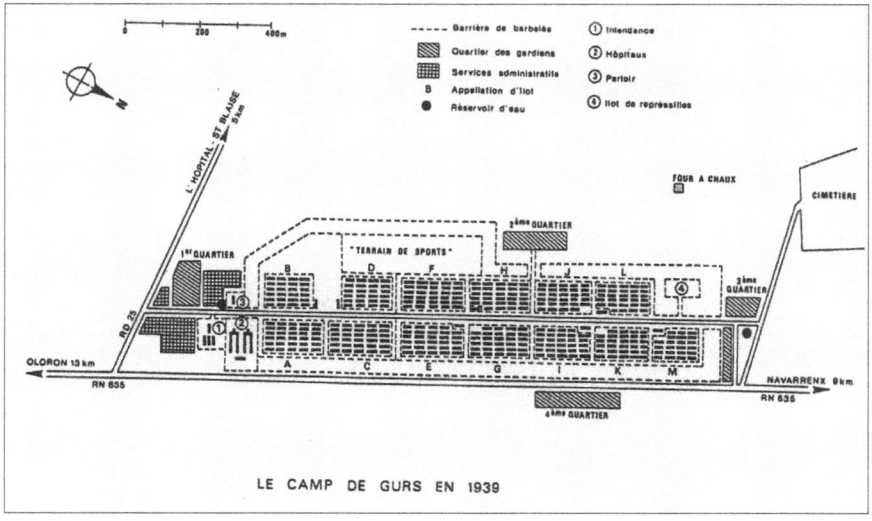

LE CAMP DE GURS EN 1939

warm socks, shoes, gloves, a warm blanket, and food. I have none of these. My previous lot was golden compared to now…..Thank God that my dear parents and my dear husband are not alive to experience this. Please help me." Klara is unaware that her passage has already been paid by Willy and Edith in September via The American Jewish Joint Distribution Committee.

Hannah Arendt, the noted Jewish philosopher is a resident of Gurs along with Albert Teutsch, the lawyer from Karlsruhe who recently traced the family's ancestors. After a few days, Klara finds her sister and brother-in-law in the camp. Her sister gives her a few items of clothing and shares some meager rations. Mail that is sent goes via Switzerland. Klara hopes that Frau Dr. Dreyfus, a family friend in Zurich can help to facilitate shipments. In early November "conditions here are miserable. I have had diarrhea but feel better now. We lie in cold barracks on straw. I have heard that people over 60 are given preference to emigrate if their papers are in order. I have gone from the frying pan into the fire. I have seen dear Helene several

An elderly internee, coping with the mud at Gurs.
*Courtesy of Centre de documentation juive contemporaine, Paris*

times. You can not imagine our sad situation." She still hopes that she will obtain her visa via Stuttgart. Her children in America have no idea where she is. They send a telegram to Frau Doktor Dreyfuss in Switzerland and finally discover their mother's address in Gurs. The mail gets through with great difficulty while war is raging in Europe. Coventry and Hamburg have been bombed. On December 30, 1940, her brother-in-law Albert Strauss collapses in the latrine and never regains consciousness. He is buried in the camp cemetery on January 1st ,1941.

While the Vichy government provides no assistance to the refugees, charitable organizations provide some necessities. Many are protestant organizations: Secours Protestant; followed by Secours Suisse and then the American Friends Service Committee known as Secours Quakers on December 28, 1940. Two Jewish organizations followed: HICEM which provided help for emigration and OSE, Oeuvres des secours aux enfants. They provided urgently needed food and some medical services. Notably absent were any catholic charities.

In a letter to her friend in Switzerland in early January 1941, she thanks her for any assistance she may be able to give. Her friend's sister is also in Gurs in another barrack where Klara meets acquaintances from Baden. The sister of her Swiss friend relates that Klara's children had sent a telegram to Switzerland and only recently discovered where she was. Even her friend has problems and tells her she can not send anything from Switzerland. Her sister's son Erich, who had fled to the south of France, has been able to assist her a bit and brought some clothing and 60 francs. On February 5, 1941, she receives the first letter from America and is overjoyed. In it she learns that their situation in America has changed. Willy's practice is not doing well, and Edith has now taken a job as a nanny for a wealthy family in a

New York suburb. They have moved out of their Port Chester home and have different addresses now.

While Erwin Rommel mounts his first attack of the North African War in March, Klara is transferred from Gurs to the hospital camp in Noe, not far from Toulouse. Just as in Germany she receives a good conduct certificate from the Director of Gurs. "I have been here for almost a month and was the only one from my barrack who got away. It is really an improvement especially as far as hygiene is concerned. I have had an attack of angina with a fever but am better again. Only a large appetite has remained. Everything here is light and bright. Unfortunately, I never received the packages you sent me but thankfully there is a canteen here." Klara is now 61 and was probably transferred to Noe due to her age and medical problems. Her younger sister Helene has found housing in a pension nearby Gurs due to the efforts of her son Erich. The Vichy government was also eager to have refugees emigrate if possible. The authorities know that Klara has children in America.

# Noe

Klara has many friends among her fellow internees at Noe. She asks Edith to try and contact relatives in New York for three of her friends who have not received any letters. She writes brief biographies of each of them and asks her daughter to look up relatives of Frieda Heimann, for Mr. and Mrs. Joseph Birnbaum, and for Karola Bermann. There is no record of successful contacts. Periodically she receives $10 from America which are exchanged for 434 francs, "but the purchasing power of the franc isn't what it used to be, and I must also pay back debts. A friend of mine helps me out here. You learn who your friends are when you are in need." By now she also realizes that her son's medical practice is in poor condition.

By the end of April Klara's letters are being censored by French security officials and stamped very much like the letters sent from Aichach. She asks that her children approach Hans Morgenthau for assistance in obtaining her visa from Marseilles. At Easter Erich and his French fiancée visited her sister Helene who was chagrined to learn that her son was marrying a catholic. They also visited Klara in Noe and she described her nephew's fiancée as delightful and beautiful.

In June Klara writes that she doesn't believe her shabby clothes will see her through another winter. The Vichy administration is also

93

placing more restrictions. Admiral Darlan, the minister of the interior, sent a memo to all the prefects of France. "I have decided that no foreigner of the Israelite race will henceforth be freed from lodging or detention centers." Helene, her younger sister, has had to return to Gurs. Her son Erich, having been in southern France for a few years, is still able to visit his mother and his aunt Klara. He frequently goes to the American Consulate in Marseilles to see whether he can expedite the visa for Klara. Meanwhile her children are struggling in America. Willy finally gave up on his practice in Port Chester and now works three days a week in a hospital in New York while trying to build-up a private practice. Edith works on commissions for a 5th Ave store for petit point and fine embroidered items. It takes her two months to finish a life size picture of Christ in petit point copying a picture of an old Italian master for a convent. Her work is much admired. She receives numerous other orders as a result.

Klara is loved and admired for her quiet dignity. She never joins in the camp gossip about others. As she tells her children "I have never made a negative statement about anyone, nor have I burdened them with my troubles. All are kind to me. We help each other as best we can." Time drags on. She has gone from riches to rags and is upset about her appearance. Periodically delayed mail arrives. The $10 she receives does not go far after she pays off debts to others first. As autumn arrives, she worries whether she will survive another winter. One of her few diversions is exchanging recipes. The notebook she bought on the long train trip from Karlsruhe has been filled with penciled notes of delicacies to be made once she is freed. For insurance she has written her last will and testament on the inside front cover. In case of death, she leaves the few things she has to her younger sister in Gurs.

The Vichy government mirrored many of Nazi Germany's decrees. Just as Goering ordered SS leader Reinhard Heydrich to speed up emigration of Jews in January of 1939, Admiral Francois Darlan encouraged emigration or repatriation of Jews in 1941. France was eager to get rid of the Israelite population. Either they could leave the country, or they had to remain confined to the camps. If a prisoner had a chance to emigrate, they were placed in holding areas while awaiting visas. As Klara waits, she becomes increasingly despondent. She doesn't believe her son is doing enough to have her obtain a visa.

Not only does America have very restrictive visa conditions, but the state department had many with strong anti-Semitic leanings.

Map reproduced courtesy of Serge Klarsfeld.
Used with permission.

France in 1940-44. The map shows the Line of Demarcation and the location of some of the principal internment camps.

The weekly broadcasts of Father Charles Edward Coughlin, which had turned strongly fascist and anti-Semitic by 1939, fanned the flames of anti- Jewish sentiment. In May of 1939 the luxury liner SS St. Louis with 900 German Jewish refugees aboard is refused at both Havana and New York and turned back to Europe. Even Roosevelt is persuaded by his state department advisors to speak of potential spies among the refugees. While Klara is trying to obtain a visa from the consulate in Marseilles, Cordell Hull the U.S. Secretary of State is reprimanding consular officials including Hiram Bingham IV of issuing too many visas to Jews. Bingham, a Yale graduate, had even visited Gurs to observe the wretched conditions. His efforts to save the Israelite refugees caused him to be abruptly removed from his position as vice consul in 1941.

On October 2, 1941, Klara receives a notice from HICEM, the Jewish emigration association, that a place has been reserved for her on a boat leaving from Lisbon pending the approval of her visa. At the same time an announcement is made that the hospital at Noe will close by the end of the year. The TB patients will be transferred to another hospital while those awaiting a visa will be transferred to a different holding site.

# Hotel Terminus

On December 6, 1941 (The day before Pearl Harbor was bombed) Klara is transferred to the Hotel Terminus in Marseilles. There she is still guarded by French gendarmes but is free to leave during the day. She sleeps in dormitory rooms which have steel bunk beds, each bed having three bunks, one above the other. She lies on the top bunk and has a linen bedsheet with two thin blankets and a pillow "in this so- called hotel". There are 28 women in the same room. Her nephew Erich comes almost daily and runs errands for many of the other internees. Shortly after she arrives in Marseilles, she passes by a store window and hardly recognized herself. "I am clothed like a beggar and can't even afford to have my shoes repaired. I am down to 55kg." Once she left the hospital in Noe, Klara has had to pay for her food. There is a small spiritus stove on which she cooks soup or an occasional vegetable. She believes that once she can leave, the boat will take her to Cuba or Mexico. Her children are having difficulty sending money as the post office refuses to accept letters with cash enclosed due to wartime regulations.

On her 63$^{rd}$ birthday December 25th Klara is invited to Christmas dinner at Erich's house. They live in a villa overlooking the Mediterranean. They spoil her by giving her citrus fruits from their garden

97

which she appreciates as she has a cold. She also receives a new warm hat, a scarf and a warm blanket and some pocket money. In the evening she returns to her cold bunk.

Throughout 1941 preparations for the final solution have been organized. In March Himmler had visited Auschwitz and ordered Kommandant Hoess (born in Baden-Baden in 1901) to expand the facility with nearby Birkenau as an additional holding area for 100,000. SS murder squads are organized in Poland. Vichy France, Romania, Hungary follow German laws. In the Ukraine more than 50,000 are murdered in Babi Yar. German Jews are now being deported to various extermination camps and in October they are no longer allowed to emigrate. By January 1942 at the Wansee conference the final solution to the Jewish problem is agreed upon. All will now be shipped east to extermination camps.

For the first 18 days of the New Year 1942 Klara has been in hospital with bronchitis. "In Gurs I was in the infirmary twice, in Noe I was in the hospital for ten months, and here I am constantly under a doctor's care. Whatever I had, I have already sold so that I could buy bread. I receive 200 francs a month support money from HICEM. Please sell a Persian rug and send me the proceeds. Erich is now jobless and only his wife can send packages to his mother." By March, French and Slovak Jews are being shipped to Auschwitz. During the day Erich now hides in the well on his wife's property near Marseilles.

On the 16th of April 1942 the Department of State sends a telegram to the American Consul in Marseilles regarding "the case of Klara Agathe Marx Herrmann". Four days later the consulate informs Klara that the authorization has been granted and that she should appear as soon as possible to complete the paperwork. "On the same day I was accompanied by a gentleman to the offices of HICEM where they immediately gave me a ticket for the ship. The next day HICEM provided me with money to send a telegram to receive my quota number and other travel documents. I also had to go to the doctor to receive a health certificate. Yesterday I went back to the consulate. My papers were in order and will be kept until the quota number is received. I paid 500 francs for the telegram. I am so happy that I will see you but won't believe it until I am on board the ship..... Beside myself about 10-12 other acquaintances have received visas. We are envied. I have received roses in congratulation and eight women cried because I will be leaving them." She also mentions that it has taken four months for the last letter to reach her. By this time Willy has given up on a private practice and signed on to the merchant marine as a ships surgeon finally earning a steady income.

On the 2nd of May 1942 Klara writes that her ship will leave Marseilles on the 10th and will transport her to Casablanca where she will wait for another ship from Lisbon since Portugal is a neutral country. On the 21st she arrives in Casablanca. Casablanca was controlled by Vichy France. It was an important assembly point for refugees. It is no coincidence that production on the movie Casablanca was just begun as Klara arrives in the fabled city. The movie is not only about refugees but many in the cast were recent refugees themselves. While Klara (spelled Clara on her documents) waits she writes a quick note to her children not knowing that she will be in Casablanca for another 18 days before the SS Serpa Pinto will arrive. She is grateful that just before she left Marseilles, she received a package sent via the Quakers containing a dress and other necessities from Edith.

The Serpa Pinto already had several working lives. With 8267 gross tons and a speed of 14 knots she wasn't the fastest boat afloat. She was

launched from Belfast in September 1914 as the Ebro for the Royal Mail Steam Packet Company. Then in 1915 she became an armed merchant cruiser. In 1919 she was converted to oil and then in 1922 sold to the Pacific Steam Navigation Company. Sold to Yugoslavia in 1935 she was renamed the Princess Olga. Then in 1940 she was sold to the Companhia Colonial de Navegacao in Lisbon and rechristened the Serpa Pinto named for a 19th century Portuguese explorer of south Africa. During World War II she was called a ship of destiny carrying 100,000 refugees to New World destinations including Rio de Janeiro, Havana, Mexico. Philadelphia and New York. Crossing the Atlantic was perilous. U-boats were watching shipping lanes and torpedoing vessels. The ship was clearly marked. The Funnel had the colors of the Portuguese flag. On its white sides the word Portugal was written in large capital letters along with a Portuguese flag. At night the ship was lit with flood lights announcing its neutrality. Looking through their periscope U-boat captains could clearly see that the vessel belonged to a neutral country. Even so, the ship was halted several times by U-boats and occasionally boarded.

On June 5th the Serpa Pinto left Lisbon for Casablanca where it would pick-up the bulk of its passengers. Originally built for 606 passengers, the ship was crammed with 677. There were 1st, 2nd, 3rd, and steerage passengers. Klara traveled in steerage class next to the boiler in a large area with steel bunk beds arranged like the bunk she had in the Hotel Terminus. She slept on the top bunk. By now she was stateless as her German passport had expired on September 12, 1941. Instead of a passport she had her quota number 1375 and visa issued by the consulate in Marseilles on April 17, 1942. On board were psychologists, doctors, diamond-cutter, housewives, students, teachers, children, engineers, artists, merchants, cabinet maker, writer, chemists, professors, composer, milliner, and journalist. Amongst its better-known passengers were Captain Pierre Dreyfus, son of the late Alfred Dreyfus, whose celebrated case of French anti-Semitism in the army caused Emile Zola to write an open letter titled J'accuse. Marcel Duchamp the well-known artist was also on board.

It took the Serpa Pinto three weeks from the time it left Lisbon till it reached America on June 25, 1942. For the better part of its transatlantic crossing, it was accompanied by two U.S. destroyers. The press release of The American Jewish Joint Distribution Committee noted that it was the 13th boat to arrive since Pearl Harbor. "The arrival of the Serpa Pinto brought to 5,200 the number of persons whom the J.D.C. has aided to escape from the Old World since America's entry into the war....Passengers said that conditions in Europe, particularly with regard to the availability of food and other necessary commodities, were becoming increasingly worse. The eyes of all Europe, they said, were upon America as the only source from which their salvation might come."

"The sailing of the Serpa Pinto was arranged by the Joint Distribution Committee which bought up all the passenger space on her. The necessary transportation funds were advanced under United States Treasury Department licenses to the J.D.C.'s American representative in Lisbon. The space was then allocated to refugees who either paid for their own passage or arranged to have relatives in the United States pay it for them." The cost for Klara's passage was $440 plus another $8 head tax. The manifest shows that Clara can read and write French and German. Her sister Helene in Gurs is listed as her relative "in the country from which the alien came from". Edith's address at 430 East 66th Street in New York is shown as her destination and the fact that her passage was paid by her children. Affidavits of the ships master and surgeon indicate that all the passengers are healthy.

# Arrival in America

On June 25, 1942 a large crowd waited anxiously on the southern tip of Manhattan. Mounted policemen kept vigil on the hot summer day. A mounted policeman's horse nibbled on the ice cream cone Edith held in her hand as she spoke to him. She scanned the arrivals looking for her mother. Finally, she saw a figure whom she didn't recognize but she recognized the dress. It was the one she had sent to Marseilles. At long last mother and daughter were reunited. As Willy had written in an earlier letter, the three leaves of a clover were together again.

Klara was lucky. A few weeks after her arrival, on July 18, 1942 SS Captain Theodore Dannecker, the chief of The Gestapo's Jewish Office in France inspects Gurs and issues orders to prepare the camps detainees for deportation to the east. Those with last names beginning A-M are to leave August 6, N-Z are to leave August 8. The women begin to weep as their names are read. In early August, during a heat wave, Klara's younger sister Helene and her sister-in-law Selma walk for three hours carrying their bags to the train station. Quakers and other aid personnel give them fruit, chocolate, and cheese. They are transported first to Drancy, a former police barracks in a northeastern suburb of Paris, and then in cattle cars to Auschwitz where they die in the gas chambers. The commandant of Auschwitz is none other than Rudolph Franz Ferdinand Hoess the boy born in Baden-Baden within a few months of Willy. Frieda Hirschhorn, one of Klara's roommates in Marseilles, along with the others who waited in vain for visas, was also transported via Drancy to Auschwitz and murdered. While eight Teutsch descendants died in Gurs and Noe, another 78 died in Auschwitz, Riga, Sobibor, and Buchenwald. These represent roughly half of those alive when Albert Teutsch wrote the family history. He was in the second transport to Auschwitz.

The family had gone from riches to rags to refugees. Willy returns from several tours in the merchant marine. When his ship was in Greenland, he treated Innuits who had come aside. One of them gives him a harpoon in gratitude for his services. On his return to New York, he works at several hospitals no longer in pediatrics but as an anesthetist. Klara is doing piecework knitting scarves. Once when she tried to board a bus with a large carton of her handiwork, the bus driver refused to admit her. She had to walk with the bulky box to deliver them. In many of the stores she could speak German, so adjustment was a bit easier. Edith had a hard time. She had been married and widowed in a short period of time. The apartments in New York were crammed with furniture.

When the war was over Willy bought two silver baskets. One for VE day and one for VJ day. The first letter from Germany came from Rudi Bader. He was in a French prisoner of war camp and asked Edith to write a letter explaining how he had helped which she of course wrote. Rudi died a few months later.

I was small but remember my tricycle being damaged by all the packages that were sent. A package filled with coffee, sugar and flour hung on each side of my handlebars. They were sent to Marie the faithful family factotum; to Frau Haas whose daughter Gerhilde had been so kind; to the Bader family and to Erich Strauss who had converted to Catholicism and was now living in Valence. Shortly after the war ended Edith's piano teacher in Baden-Baden wrote that her Bechstein grand piano was found in the house of tax inspector Schaubeck the one who had stipulated that the swastika seals be kept on the piano. A disgruntled mob threw the piano out of the window of the apparently reviled inspector's house. Although Baden-Baden was now in the French zone of occupation, a small detachment of American military briefly occupied Villa Edith, Schillerstrasse 19, and made it their local headquarters. When they discovered the house was owned by Americans, they left leaving the stately villa in disrepair. The villas were returned to the family and then sold for a song in the early fifties.

By now the family had moved to Chicago. Willy worked at the American Hospital along with many other European and Nationalist Chinese emigres. He also worked at Rush Presbyterian St Luke's and a few days a week at Downey Veterans Hospital at Great Lakes Naval Station. Whenever he could he played his cello in chamber music ensembles with fellow doctors. With familiar furniture and the oil portraits of the family surrounding them they could imagine they were still in the villa instead of a small townhouse. He was the first to die at 51. Klara died a few years later in 1956. She never spoke about her experiences. She kept the same stoic silence which served her well in her captivity. The area, which is called Roscoe Village in Chicago today, had many stores owned by Germans. German was spoken both by the butchers and the bakers. The doctors said she had hardening of the arteries which resulted in dementia. In the last six years of her life Klara was confused and unsure of her whereabouts.

Edith continued to struggle to make ends meet. She worked at numerous jobs as secretary or bookkeeper. From time to time, she still sat at the piano and sang the German lieder of Schubert and Brahms. Most of the time she was typing away furiously, addressing letters to her German lawyers seeking restitution for the items that were stolen. It did not help her blood pressure. Every time she typed a letter, she remembered her years of deprivation and degradation. In the end the Wiedergutmachung (literally the making good again or restitution) merely enriched the lawyers and very little accrued to her benefit. The night before she died, she sat at the piano and sang a song from The Farewell Waltz based on the haunting Chopin melody. She was 65. The sheet music from the last movie she saw in Germany was still on the piano when she died on a beautiful day in May.

# Epilogue

In retrospect I understand my family much better now. My grandmother used to say there was nothing better than a good dark rye bread with butter. After years of deprivation, it was the simplest things that made her happy. She read the Aufbau, a German newspaper primarily written for German Jewish refugees with articles by Hannah Arendt (a fellow Gurs prisoner), Thomas Mann, Albert Einstein, and Stefan Zweig. In Chicago there was the Abendpost, a German newspaper begun in 1889 which existed until 1950. Her doctor was a German émigré who actually made house calls. Most of her relatives and friends had been murdered. There was a melancholy in her eyes which saw everything and nothing. Frequently she seemed to stare right out into infinity. What did she see there? Did she see her father giving her five pfennigs to buy a glass of beer on her fifth birthday? Did she see the prison warden who wouldn't let her read her daughter's letter? Did she see the false accusers who had denounced her? Did she see her younger sister Helene trudging back to the train station in Oloron to be shipped to Drancy and from there to Auschwitz? Did she remember the Belle Epoch before the first world war when she entertained artists and aristocrats, businessmen and diplomats in Villa Edith?

I now realize that I was raised in a house with many ghosts. The past haunted our environment. Although I watched as my mother read her prayer books, my family didn't belong to any institutionalized religion. We kept quiet. My family feared organized religion having lost their cultural home because of it. They loved the cloak of anonymity that America gave them especially in a large city like Chicago. They taught me to stand up for the underdog in society, for the oppressed for those who had very little and were misunderstood. The McCarthy era frightened them. A few weeks before my mother died there were the Kent State killings where four students died when Ohio State National Guard shot them as they protested the Vietnam war. As she saw dissenting voices being stilled, my mother was frightened anew. She knew democracy was fragile and could easily be broken. From her own experience she knew that tyrants twist public opinion and can rig the court system. Whenever she watched a Perry Mason drama on TV, she empathized with the accused. I didn't understand then why she would get so upset. But now I realize those shows brought back memories of her own trials.

My mother never held a job for very long. In hindsight I realize she was always a bit paranoid, and feared others were out to get her. As a single mother she never stopped working as after my uncle died, she became the main bread winner. From time to time, to pay for my education, she would pawn her jewelry. The pawnshop knew her so well that they gave her a reduced rate and she always redeemed what she pawned. Now I know she had learned how to do this in the difficult years after 1935. Both my mother and uncle suffered pangs of guilt having left Germany leaving my grandmother to suffer the indignities that she did.

As a child I must have absorbed some of their fears. One of the most fearsome questions from my classmates was, "What religion are you?" It was a question I couldn't answer although I sometimes went alone to The Peoples Church in Chicago and sat on Preston Bradley's knee during Sunday school. There were an untold number of epithets that my classmates used about Jews. I winced when I heard them but kept quiet. I didn't learn about sports since no one in my family knew anything about American sports. I grew up in a mainly catholic area with classmates of German, Irish and Italian descent. In a way I was always the outsider just as my family was and had been even in Germany.

In October of 2013 I visited an old and forgotten Jewish cemetery in search of my ancestors on the outskirts of a small Palatinate village of Essingen. There I met a kind local resident who seemed to be the unofficial guardian of the ancient site. He had obtained the key to the cemetery from the village hall and accompanied me to the hallowed ground. On either side the cemetery is surrounded by vineyards. We discovered the gravesite of Jakob Teutsch I and other ancestors

described by Albert Teutsch in his family genealogy tables. We also witnessed the recent desecration of a number of the gravestones. Someone had painted the ancient appellation of "Sau Jude" (dirty Jew) across several gravestones a silent echo of Martin Luther and Adolph Hitler. The majority of the dead had died in the 18th and 19th century. How could they have possibly disturbed anyone today? Past prejudices seem to persist in the present.

History is not supposed to repeat itself but sometimes I wonder.

# Bibliography

## Books

Arendt, Hannah: *Eichmann in Jerusalem: A Report on the Banality of Evil,* 1963

Frojmovic, Eva ed.: *Imaging the Self, Imaging the Other: Visual Representations and Jewish-Christian Dynamics in the Middle and Early Modern Period:* 2003 Brill

Hoess, Rudolph: *Death Dealer: Memoirs of the SS Komanndant at Auschwitz*, Prometheus Books 1992

Kuller, Christiane; Finanzverwaltung und Judenverfolgung, Munich 2008

Kershaw, Ian: *Hitler: a biography* 1998

Laharie, Claude : *Le Camp de Gurs*, 1993 Société Atlantique d'Impression à Biarritz

Larson, Erik: *In the Garden of the Beasts: Love, Terror, and an American Family in Hitler's Berlin:* Crown Publishers 2011

Miller, Richard Lawrence: *Nazi Justiz: law of the Holocaust*: 1995 Praeger Publishers

Muller, Ingo: *Hitler's Justice, The Courts of the Third Reich*: 1991 Harvard University Press

Reuter, Fritz: *WARMAISA 1000 Jahren Juden in Worms*: 1987 Athenaeum Verlag GmbH

Schindler, Angelika: *Der verbrannte Traum: Juedische Burger und Gaeste in Baden-Baden*: 1992 Elster

Schleunes, Karl A.: *The Twisted Road to Auschwitz*: 1970 University of Illinois Press

Schorn, Hubert: *Die gesetzgebung des Nationalsozialismus als Mittel der Macht*: 1963 v. Klostermann

Strickland, Debra Higgs: *Saracens, Demons & Jews:*

Wachsmann, Nikolaus: *Hitler's Prisons: Legal Terror in Nazi Germany*: 2004 Yale University Press

Wuellenweber, Hans: *Sondergerichte im Dritten Reich: vergessene Verbrechen der Justiz*: 1990

Frankfurt a.m. Luchterhand

Zuccotti, Susan: *The Holocaust, The French, And the Jews*: 1993 Basic Books

## Documents and Letters

Wuert. Landesstrafanstalt Gotteszell, Personal Akten der Gefangenen Edith Herrmann file 2194 49 pages

300-page Aichach Dossier from Munich Archives on CD

Herrmann, Klara private letters from Aichach, Gurs, Noe, Marseilles, and Casa Blanca

Herrmann, Edith private letters from Baden-Baden, Port Chester, and New York

Official documents from German, French and American authorities

www.ingramcontent.com/pod-product-compliance
Lightning Source LLC
Chambersburg PA
CBHW051538120626
46551CB00013B/1273